D1083917

the early poetry of **JAROSLAV SEIFERT**

the early poetry of **Jaroslav**

Seifert

City in Tears, Sheer Love,

On the Waves of TSF, and

The Nightingale Sings Poorly

TRANSLATED BY Dana Loewy

Hydra Books Northwestern University Press Evanston, Illinois

Hydra Books
Northwestern University Press
Evanston, Illinois 60208-4210

City in Tears originally published in Czech in 1921 under the title *Město v slzách: první verše* by R. Rejman, Prague. *Sheer Love* originally published in Czech in 1923 under the title *Samá láska* by Večernice/V. Vortel, R. Rejman, Prague. *On the Waves of TSF* originally published in Czech in 1925 under the title *Na vlnách TSF* by Václav Petr, Prague. *The Nightingale Sings Poorly* originally published in Czech in 1926 under the title *Slavík zpívá špatně* by Odeon, Prague. English translation copyright © 1997 by Dana Loewy.
Compilation copyright © 1997 by Hydra Books/Northwestern University Press. Published 1997 by arrangement with Jana Seifertová.

Printed in the United States of America

ISBN 0-8101-1383-X

Library of Congress
Cataloging-in-Publication Data

Seifert, Jaroslav, 1901–
[Poems. English. Selections]
The early poetry of Jaroslav Seifert / translated by Dana Loewy.
p. cm.
ISBN 0-8101-1383-X (cloth : alk. paper)
I. Loewy, Dana. II. Title.
PG5038.S45A23   1997
891.8′6152—dc21   97-10503
                              CIP

The paper used in this publication meets the minimum requirements of the American National Standard for Information Sciences—Permanence of Paper for Printed Library Materials, ANSI Z39.48-1984.

Contents

THE NIGHTINGALE SINGS POORLY

I

Translator's Notes and Acknowledgments

I have used the following editions of Seifert's texts as the basis for my translations: *City in Tears: Město v slzách: první verše* (Prague: R. Rejman, 1921); *Sheer Love: Samá láska* (Prague: Večernice/ V. Vortel, R. Rejman, 1923); *On the Waves of TSF: Na vlnách TSF* (Prague: Václav Petr, 1925); *The Nightingale Sings Poorly: Slavík zpívá špatně* (Prague: Odeon, 1926).

* * *

I would like to thank the three individuals who directly inspired this project: Moshe Lazar, professor of comparative literature at the University of Southern California, and my friends and colleagues Pamela Gilbert and Robert Johnson. Jay Martin, David St. John, and Michael Heim were my patient mentors, advisors, and critics at all stages of this undertaking. I am immensely grateful for the support of Jaroslav Seifert's daughter, Jana Seifertová-Plichtová, who shared memories of her late father with me on several occasions. The American Literary Translators Association has encouraged me with its collegial atmosphere. Two travel awards allowed me to attend ALTA's annual conferences, where I could "test" work in progress on a live audience of translators. I owe thanks to my editors at Northwestern University Press, in particular Susan Harris and Ellen Feldman. Finally, I am indebted to my parents, Dana and Georg Loewy, who not only gave me their unflagging moral support but also provided valuable linguistic and research assistance.

Introduction *Dana Loewy*

Despite his considerable stature as a Nobel Laureate and contrary to his immense popularity in the former Czechoslovakia, the present Czech Republic, Jaroslav Seifert (1901–86) has yet to become the subject of systematic English-language critical study. Since the early 1930s, Seifert has been a household name in his homeland, where to this day new editions of his verse sell in record numbers. At least since the early 1970s, world-renowned Slavic scholars have championed Seifert. In 1984 the Nobel Prize committee recognized his lifetime achievement, which encompasses six decades during which he produced several dozen volumes of poetry, some translations, and a prose memoir. Yet Seifert remains a largely unknown quantity in English-speaking countries. This paradox is due in part to the lack of quality translations available at the time the Nobel Prize was awarded; thereafter, the interest of the poetry-reading audience may have diminished because most of the renditions that sought to capitalize on Seifert's sudden international fame fell short of expectations kindled by such global literary recognition. In the absence of intriguing English versions of Seifert's poetry, critics outside Czechoslovakia largely ignored the 1984 Nobel Prize winner.

As I have tried to show elsewhere (Loewy 1995a, 1995b), the most damaging translations were authored by Paul Jagasich and Tom O'Grady. Their renderings of *The Casting of Bells* (1983), *Mozart in Prague: Thirteen Rondels* (1985), and *Dressed in Light* (1990), while well-intentioned, reveal the translators' grave linguistic deficiencies, resulting in misunderstandings, inaccuracies, and downright misrepresentations of Seifert's art. However, even the linguistically accurate translations available today fail to satisfy from the standpoint of aesthetics and poetic authenticity. Lyn Coffin's translation of *The Plague Monument* (1980) strikes the reader as at times awkward and wordy. J. K. Klement's and Eva Stucke's rendering of *A Wreath of Sonnets* (1987), a volume meant to acquaint the English-speaking world "with the true Seifert," is a complex serial poem that offers a formidable technical challenge, but, despite its formal rigor, it is arguably not representative of Seifert's work as a whole. Klement and Stucke clearly value form above all other artistic means, since formal characteristics, to them, apparently most reassuringly define what poetry is. Hence, they seem willing to sacrifice lexical choices and meaning to form, leading to inevitable padding. Even the most memorable and informative Seifert anthology to date, *The Selected Poetry of Jaroslav Seifert* (1986), edited by George Gibian with translations by Ewald Osers, generally lacks the vividness and poetic quality of Seifert's original. The same applies to Osers's other major Seifert translations: *The Plague Column* (1979) and *An Umbrella from Piccadilly* (1983).

It has often been claimed, as Gibian does in his preface to *The Selected Poetry of Jaroslav Seifert*, that only Seifert's "mature" and late work can be safely translated: "The poems of Seifert's early and middle periods often depended so heavily on effects of sound that they lose much of their quality in translation or are altogether untranslatable" (Gibian 1986, 14). Apart from the fact that this precept effectively rules out thirty years of the poet's most prolific and interesting literary endeavor—that is, anything written between 1920 and 1950—Seifert's musicality, playfulness, and lyricism can be imitated in English with the help of internal rhymes, half-rhymes, and assonance, although, of course, some features will inevitably be lost. Without a doubt, it is easier to translate the later Seifert than the earlier Seifert because he increasingly dispensed with formal modes, such as rhyme and strict rhythmic patterns, and came to rely less and less on paronomastic means, such as puns and wordplay. The playfulness of his early poetry, particularly in *On the Waves of TSF* and *The Nightingale Sings Poorly,* is evidenced in anecdotes and witty aphorisms. Seifert relied, too, on such sound patterns as alliteration, assonance, and euphony in general. These features *can* be imitated in English, and the sensuality, eroticism, epicureanism, wit, and humor of Seifert's early work can be recreated and conveyed to the English-speaking reader, as I hope my own translations will demonstrate. Moreover, I hope to show that

Seifert's early poetry has a specific historical value as a piece of the modernist puzzle in the Europe of the 1920s.

Jaroslav Seifert was born on September 23, 1901 in Žižkov, a working-class neighborhood of Prague. It is this environment that richly informed not only his early poetry but his mature work, despite the fact that in June 1938 he moved to the quiet and idyllic suburb of Břevnov, where he would live until his death. In his memoir *Všecky krásy světa* [All the beauties of the world] (1981), Seifert frequently harks back to his Žižkov youth in what was then the Austro-Hungarian Empire. He recalls a life of poverty and want, even as he records the experience, rich in sensual impressions, that fueled his abundant imagination. He attempts to perceive the lyricism of the everyday squalor and feels closely tied to Žižkov because it was a place of initiation, most prominently into romantic and erotic love, which for Seifert are inseparable. This gradual discovery is shrouded in mystery in the naive youngster's vision; and one reason for Seifert's lasting charm may be the fact that both in his life and in his works, he retained some of this innocent naïveté and sense of awe.

Though Seifert's family suffered genuine hardship, his wonder and basically sunny disposition are noticeable even in accounts of the more difficult moments of his Žižkov youth. He describes the densely populated, squalid tenement blocks from the nineteenth century, built for commercial profit and speculation and without much consideration for their occupants. In recalling the "mournful melody of decay and the smell of poverty" in which people struggled for their meager happiness, he declares, "I fell in love with even the uninviting dead-end streets, full of dust, soot, and lousy grass between cobblestones" (Seifert 1981, 88). Žižkov was teeming with pubs and wine bars; there was one in every four or five houses. As a boy, Seifert would sit on neighborhood steps with his friends, watching the drunks and listening with keen interest and curiosity to their sentimental love songs and rowdy tunes. Seifert's mother, a devout Catholic, tried to counter this influence with attendance at evening mass and baroque church hymns. Seifert admits that powerful inspiration for his future poetry sprang from these disparate sources (Seifert 1981, 181).

Seifert's parents apparently tolerated the various worlds of the poet's early experience. His mother, "a quiet, lyrical Catholic, heeding God's laws and those of the Church," shook off the grim daily routine by attending mass. Religion, Seifert writes, "was her poetry" (Seifert 1981, 283). His father was a Social Democrat and atheist, often taking his son to rallies and party meetings. The Czech literary scholar Zdeněk Pešat convincingly argues that the happy coexistence of these two influences profoundly impressed themselves on Seifert and ensured that the poet was never prone to radical excesses, in either his life or his work, but always strove to reconcile differences and to harmonize extremes (Pešat 1991, 10). Certainly, the young boy moved between the two worlds effortlessly, sometimes intoning socialist songs at political meetings or attending rallies immediately after singing long Marian hymns and standing next to his mother in the church pew.

Seifert came of age in a time of political turmoil and was subject to diverse influences that eventually shaped his political orientation. The first Czechoslovak Republic formed in 1918; only two years later strikes would mask an unsuccessful communist coup attempt. However, the imposing figure of the popular first president, Tomáš Garrigue Masaryk (1918–35), guaranteed a high degree of continuity and stability, even after the world economic crisis in 1929. The new republic's constitution was centralist like its French model, and France was also its most important political ally. Nevertheless, even this democratic government struggled with labor unrest and social upheaval, partly fueled by communist forces; the government resorted to censorship against the radical press. This volatile political situation informs most of the "proletarian" poetry in Seifert's first and second collections, *The City in Tears* (1921) and *Sheer Love* (1923).

In 1920 the Social Democratic Party split into a moderate democratic faction and a radical Bolshevik wing. The latter adhered to the idea of a class struggle, modeling itself after the

Soviets; in 1921 it officially became the Communist Party with its own newspaper, *Rudé právo,* to which Seifert frequently contributed throughout the 1920s. The 1917 October Revolution and glowing first accounts of the sweeping changes in Russia energized leftish-leaning intellectuals. Revolutionary poetry by Aleksandr Blok and Vladimir Mayakovsky appeared in print (Seifert himself translated Blok's long poem *The Twelve* with the help of Roman Jakobson).

But there were other, even more important, influences. Around 1920 the Czech avant-garde, led by its chief theoretician, the graphic artist Karel Teige, began to discover Guillaume Apollinaire; and in 1920 the playwright, novelist, and critic Karel Čapek published his brilliantly translated anthology of modern French poets, *Francouzská poezie nové doby.* Both events had a profound effect on the development of the new Czech poetry. So did recent developments in the fine arts: Cubism, Futurism, Dadaism, as well as the naive paintings of Henri Rousseau. In his memoir, Seifert recalls the important impact of Apollinaire's poetry, how struck he was by *Zône* and *Alcools* (Seifert 1981, 289). The eminent Czech literary critic and writer F. X. Šalda encouraged Seifert to explore older French poets, and particularly to try his hand at translating Verlaine, which Seifert did most extensively between 1929 and 1933.

There were other important influences as well: Czech poets of the late nineteenth century, the previous poetic generation, and Seifert's own literary peers. At the outset of his career, during the early 1920s, he was strongly under the sway of S. K. Neumann and the program of so-called proletarian poetry, but later gravitated toward Karel Teige and his "poetist" conception of modern art. In Seifert's recollection, this decade seems an endless stream of daily meetings and heated debates about art, literature, and politics in Prague's many literary cafés and wine bars. Some of his friends wrote, translated, or composed at cafés; they had "their" tables there, and could be found there day in and day out.

The avant-garde artistic association Devětsil initially arose in late 1920 from Teige's programmatic theses, which then were entirely identical with proletarian art but later evolved into a uniquely Czech modernist movement, "poetism." Devět-sil increasingly began to unite artists on ideological grounds, most prominently communists, and its membership fluctuated strongly (Pešat 1991, 17). Devětsil (literally "nine power") is the Czech name for butterbur, the "mysterious and singular medicinal herb which in its name bears the magical number nine." According to Seifert (accounts of the association's inception vary), the name was chosen by the founding members who happened to number nine, among them two painters and two architects. The artists had discovered the herb in a recent book by the brothers Josef and Karel Čapek (Seifert 1981, 152).

Karel Teige, only a year older than Seifert, was instrumental in the poet's early development, and Seifert acknowledged on several occasions how much he admired Teige's erudition and liked his personality. Seifert credits Teige with expanding Apollinaire's readership in Prague after Čapek introduced him to Czech readers in his famous translations. Seifert suggests that the immensely rich crop of poets and writers of his time should rightly be called "Teige's generation" to acknowledge the impact of Teige, now largely unjustly forgotten. The two men saw each other almost daily, either in Teige's large home library, where the first Devětsil meetings were also held, or in one of the many cafés they frequented. It was Teige, Seifert says, who opened the world of art for him, particularly in light of the poet's insufficient proficiency in foreign tongues (Seifert 1981, 151, 446). Teige apparently taught him to appreciate poetry as well as the fine arts. Teige wrote authoritative essays on art, literature, film, and architecture, among other things. His command of French was excellent, and he knew a great deal of modern poetry by heart. Seifert reminisces how he first heard Teige recite Apollinaire's "Sous le pont Mirabeau" and Verlaine's poetry in the original the day they met. It was also Teige who took Seifert on his first trip to Italy and France in 1923, to familiarize the poet with modern art as he rigorously defined it.

During this same period in the early 1920s, Seifert began his long journalistic career, although he remained passionate about literature and poetry. He wrote reviews of plays, books, films, and lectures. Over the course of the decade, Seifert would turn from youthful experimentation and the naive absorption of several crucial influences to the formation of a style that was entirely an individualistic expression of his own personality. This development can be traced from each collection of poetry in this volume to the next. Seifert's finding of his own voice, perhaps not surprisingly, coincided with his expulsion from the Communist Party and his break with Devětsil in 1929.

Poetism—the denial of established art and the celebration of everyday objects or popular entertainment like the circus, film, and dance halls—was not a traditional artistic program but a way of perceiving the world that was to become poetry itself. It was to be the art of life, the ability to live and enjoy. (Such lighthearted escape from engagé art, from proletarian poetry, is perhaps not surprising given the recent end of World War I.) Seifert recalls that during his trip to Paris with Teige, in 1923, he was forced to sneak into the Louvre secretly, because Teige respected nothing but ultramodern art and what he perceived as its immediate precursors. For Teige, modern art was conceived in the circus, on the cinema screen, or along the brightly illuminated boulevards with their neon signs. Teige passed the Louvre, state-sponsored theaters, libraries, and museums with disdain. To him they were temples of exclusive taste where art was destined to die in obscurity. But waxworks, galleries selling contemporary paintings, the Folies Bergères, jazz bands, cafés, and music halls were a must. Similarly, Charlie Chaplin, Douglas Fairbanks, and other actors and "popular" artists were elevated to the status of cult figures. The poetists adopted Ilya Ehrenburg's motto that the new modern art ceased to be art. Both as a modernist movement and as a "way of life," poetism was characterized by its playfulness and unfettered creativity; it stressed emotion and imagination over logic, accompanied by formal looseness: casual, irregular rhyme patterns, slant rhymes, colloquialism, wordplay. Poetism is an eclectic amalgam of Futurist, Dadaist, and Constructivist elements, yet, as this volume shows, it is also a uniquely Czech movement.

In his second collection of poetry, *Sheer Love* (1923), Seifert not only reflected elements of this artistic conception but in turn apparently influenced Teige's poetist theses (Pešat 1991, 48–49). Poetism, therefore, was essentially congenial to Seifert's nature—perhaps more so than to Teige's. The poet's sympathy for the suffering of the poor never diminished, but his vision was more differentiated than proletarian poetry's stern propagandistic insistence on class struggle would allow. His unpretentious proletarianism was innate, not acquired, and to an extent shaped his life vision. Poetism, as Teige conceived it, attracted many new members to Devětsil and shaped Czech poetry in the mid-1920s. Its task was to extol and to encompass "all the beauties of the world"—the functional symbols of modernity, such as machines, electric light, skyscrapers—as the final poem in the collection *Sheer Love* suggests both in title and in content. It is interesting that Seifert chose this same title for his prose memoir, thus nostalgically returning to the time of his youthful experimentation.

Seifert's third collection, *On the Waves of TSF* (1925), is entirely in the poetist vein. It is the quintessential expression of the movement, the most consistent application of "poetry as play" (Pešat 1991, 61), although this does not mean that it disregards serious themes entirely. The playful element is evident even in the book's flippant dedication to Seifert's poetist friends, all innovators in their respective fields: fellow poet Vítězslav Nezval, who helped conceive and apply poetism in his own work; Jindřich Honzl, one of the founders of avant-garde theater; and, of course, Karel Teige. It is in Teige's typography that poetist playfulness is expressed most prominently in Seifert's work. Like László Moholy-Nagy, Teige believed that typography not only complements a text, but that it becomes an important means of expression in its own right. Almost every poem in *On the Waves of TSF* is set in a different typeface, in varying sizes. This graphic layout underscores the whimsical nature of many poems; so does the poet's attempt to depict the fascinating phenomena of the modern world as he witnessed them on his recent trip to France. Seifert's debt to Apollinaire and to modern poetry is evident. The unconventional graphics are part of a provocative, irreverent gesture that culminates in his printing the name of a brand of condoms—Ollagum—next to the poem "Nightlights." Echoes of E. F. T. Marinetti are not coincidental in Seifert's work, as the Italian Futurist visited Prague and Devětsil on several occasions. In late 1926 Seifert published *The Nightingale Sings Poorly,* which continues and even perfects semantic play while already inaugurating a different, a more wistful tone. Here as well Seifert excels at associative word combinations that rely heavily on the resources of the Czech language and present a great challenge to the translator. Several poems at the end of the collection reflect Seifert's 1925 trip to the Soviet Union, which he undertook as part of an official delegation with Teige and other writers and intellectuals, for the Society for Economic and Cultural Friendship with the New Russia. Seifert's response to this journey seems mixed. His verse suggests that he was not oblivious to the turmoil and violence in postrevolutionary Russia, despite his early revolutionary zeal. There is no mention of this visit in his memoirs. In January 1928, after several years of acquaintance and romantic involvement, Seifert married Marie Ulrychová from Jičín, a town that figures prominently in *Sheer Love.* A year later a rare prose publication, *Hvězdy nad Rajskou zahradou* [The stars above paradise], appeared, consisting of autobiographical pieces that look back humorously at the author's childhood, coming of age, and artistic affiliations during the 1920s. Seifert's retrospective orientation signals the beginning of a new phase.

The year 1929 marks a turning point for Seifert. Most critics, foremost among them Zdeněk Pešat, agree that the collection *Carrier Pigeon* manifests a poetic transition that foreshadows Seifert's mature work of the 1930s. Although the poet still maintains his preoccupation with external sensory details, this collection initiates a trend toward internalization and intimacy (Pešat 1991, 77). His political disillusionment is evident; revolutionary fervor is replaced by skepticism. As the 1920s progressed, Devětsil gradually turned dogmatic, even Stalinist; it no longer provided Seifert with creative inspiration (Seifert 1991, 445). In 1929 Seifert, along with six other writers, signed a letter of protest against the policies of the new pro-Stalinist party leadership of

Klement Gottwald and was subsequently expelled from the Czechoslovak Communist Party. As a result, he was also barred professionally from the party press, to which he had contributed throughout the decade. As became evident in the hard-line 1950s, the Communist Party would not forgive Seifert's deviation, especially since he always stood by his decision and yet never ceased to adhere to moderately leftist Social Democratic ideas. During the 1930s he often entered into polemical battles with members of the radical left, mainly with Julius Fučík.

In 1938 Czechoslovakia fell victim to Hitler's aggression. France, Czechoslovakia's ally along with Great Britain, succumbed to Germany's pressure and ceded the Sudetenland, mainly inhabited by the German minority, to the Nazis. The infamous Munich Treaty failed to secure peace in Europe and to stop Hitler's expansion. Rather, it paved the way for Germany's incorporation of the remaining Czech lands into the Reich as the "Protectorate Bohemia and Moravia" in March 1939. Slovakia became a puppet state dominated by Germany. Seifert responded to the threat to Czech political and cultural sovereignty in his rousing collection *Zhasněte světla* [Put out the lights], published in late 1938, again to considerable acclaim and readership. The poet assumed the responsibility to act as a spokesman of his people, particularly in times of imminent danger to nationhood. The collection, much like Seifert's wartime verse, invokes Czech history and cultural icons to remind the readers of past resilience and overcoming of national catastrophes. In this deeply lyrical volume, Seifert eroticizes his native land. With this sincere, natural, and intimate expression of what the Czech people felt and needed, Seifert assumed the role he had long cherished— that of the revolutionary bard who would lead the masses on the barricades.

Seifert's human decency and courage came to the fore during the period of de-Stalinization in 1956 at the Second Writers Congress. He was the only one to come out in support of imprisoned and silenced colleagues, and to demand their rehabilitation (Hejl 1984, 100). In the speech he made there, he stressed honesty, thus echoing his early classical idea of the poet as Aristotelian truth-giver and truth-maker: "When anyone else keeps the truth to himself, it can be a tactical maneuver. If the writer keeps the truth to himself, he is lying." He went on to say: "It is wonderful if poets are prodding politicians, but I dare say that it is less wonderful when it is the other way around" (Pešat 1991, 188).

Due to the continuing political relaxation in the course of the 1960s, it was finally possible to accord Jaroslav Seifert the official recognition he had earned long ago: he was named National Artist in 1966. Before the Warsaw Pact invasion of Czechoslovakia on August 21, 1968 crushed the hopes for reform and "socialism with a human face," Seifert published two collections of poetry in quick succession: *Halleyova kometa* [Halley's comet] and *Odlévání zvonů* [The casting of bells] (1967). Both are characterized by diction that is increasingly proselike. Thematically, erotic love and femininity return; so does confessional and contemplative verse as well as reminiscence. The invasion and subsequent military occupation of Czechoslovakia cut short the time Seifert could devote to his next collection, *Morový sloup* [The plague column]. He thought of this book as his last and conceived it to a great extent as a parting gesture. Love, aging, and death are central themes; so is poetic stock-taking at the end of a long, rich, difficult life.

During this new national crisis Seifert again did not hesitate to take on the responsibility that followed from his standing as "the conscience of the nation." He was elected chairman of the Czech Writers Association at its 1968 congress and led a task force in the national writers association (which included both Czech and Slovak writers) to rehabilitate authors persecuted under the previous Communist regime. The novelist Milan Kundera remembers Seifert's authority and unbending stance:

I keep seeing him before me. He walked with difficulty, on crutches. And perhaps due to the illness, when he was sitting, he seemed like a rock: immovable, solid, firm. We felt relief, when he was with us. What justification of existence can a small doomed nation give? The justification was here: the poet, square-shouldered, crutches leaning against the table, the tangible proof of the genius of the nation, the only glory of the powerless. (Kundera 1984, 53)

Seifert's collection *The Plague Column*, circulated in samizdat typescripts, first appeared in a German exile edition in 1977 and was later published in Czechoslovakia in 1981. The new hard-line regime was often at a loss for how to deal with the poet, whose authority in his homeland as well as abroad continued to increase, even though his new works could not be published—except for *Deštník z Piccadilly* [An umbrella from Piccadilly] (1979), which had been copied and circulated since 1978, but about which critics were not allowed to write. In this collection Seifert maintained his inner autonomy and continued in his contemplative, reminiscing vein, acknowledging the inevitable proximity of love and death and anticipating the latter almost longingly.

Seifert's popularity, moral authority, and international acclaim among literary insiders granted him a certain immunity to intervene on behalf of human rights causes, most importantly, the signing of Charter 77 in 1977. The 1984 Nobel Prize for literature embarrassed a regime that would have preferred to ignore the international attention the award generated. Seifert's last collection, *Býti básníkem* [To be a poet] (1983), continued the confessional character of his previous book and exuded a calm, resigned attitude toward life and impending death. For the last time the poet celebrated the city of Prague. On January 10, 1986, Seifert died and was buried in the town of Kralupy near Prague. His funeral drew large crowds of mourners (and consequently the attention of the police).

In his congratulatory letter, dated October 11, 1984, on the occasion of the Nobel Prize award to Seifert, then-playwright and dissident Václav Havel succinctly formulated the reasons why the poet had long deserved this honor:

Not only because your poetic work has long . . . become common property, that is, everyone who is the least bit interested in literature got it under his skin, so to say; not only because you have long been something of a living symbol of the continuity in modern Czech literature; but also because with your moral stance—unpretentious and all the more lasting—you embody the best tradition of a responsible civic stance of a writer in this country. (Havel 1984, 104)

Despite the turbulence in his life, some aspects of the poet's sensibility and life remained remarkably constant: his deep, natural rootedness in his proletarian origins; his ability to address universally shared human experiences, like love and death, in an accessible yet profoundly relevant manner; his simple appetites and reliance on the senses; and his lifelong ties to the place of his birth, to Prague, to the Czech lands, devoid of pathos or fanatical nationalism.

WORKS CITED

Čapek, Karel, ed. and trans. [1920] 1968. *Francouzská poezie nové doby*. Prague: Československý spisovatel.

Gibian, George. 1986. Preface to *The Selected Poetry of Jaroslav Seifert*. In Seifert 1986, 1–18.

Havel, Václav. 1984. "Dopis Jaroslavu Seifertovi." In Seifert 1984, 104.

Hejl, Vilém. 1984. "Přílohy k nevydanému zatykači." In Seifert 1984, 100–102.

Kundera, Milan. 1984. "Bylo jich pět." In Seifert 1984, 52–53.

Loewy, Dana. 1995a. "The Early Poetry of Jaroslav Seifert: Translation Theory and Practice." Ph.D. diss., University of Southern California.

———. 1995b. "The Translator as Traitor: The Strange Doing of Paul Jagasich." *Translation Review* 48 (October): 39–49.

Pešat, Zdeněk. 1991. *Jaroslav Seifert*. Prague: Československý spisovatel.

Seifert, Jaroslav. 1929. *Hvězdy nad Rajskou zahradou*. Prague: Pokrok.

———. 1979. *The Plague Column*. Trans. Ewald Osers. London and Boston: Terra Nova.

———. 1980. *Morový sloup. The Plague Monument*. Trans. Lyn Coffin. N.p.: SVU Press. [Dual language]

———. 1981. *Všecky krásy světa: Příběhy a vzpomínky*. Cologne: Index.

———. 1983a. *The Casting of Bells*. Trans. Paul Jagasich and Tom O'Grady. Iowa City: The Spirit That Moves Us Press.

———. 1983b. *An Umbrella from Piccadilly*. Trans. Ewald Osers. London: Magazine Editions.

———. 1984. *Knížka polibků*. Ed. Dagmar Eisnerová. Zurich: Konfrontace.

———. 1985. *Mozart in Prague: Thirteen Rondels*. Trans. Paul Jagasich and Tom O'Grady. Iowa City: The Spirit That Moves Us Press.

———. 1986. *The Selected Poetry of Jaroslav Seifert*. Ed. George Gibian. Trans. Ewald Osers. London: André Deutsch.

———. 1987. *A Wreath of Sonnets. Věnec sonetů*. Trans. J. K. Klement and Eva Stucke. Toronto: Lakewood Books/Sixty-Eight Publishers. [Dual language]

———. 1990. *Dressed in Light*. Trans. Paul Jagasich and Tom O'Grady. New York and Baltimore: Dolphin-Moon Press.

City in Tears

1921

To the Dearest Among Poets St. K. Neumann

Foreword

A poem is not a phantasm, but a difficult and inconsiderable achievement like a workman's labor. The Revolution pervades the world; the new order of production is setting in. Our time rumbles with the explosions of wars, class struggles, the fall of civilization, and a communist world is being born in chaos as it reigned at the beginning of the earth. Witty and silly fabrications of men of letters count for nothing. Yes and no, your approval, comrade, and your defiance are voiced in this book of verse, and all that is from your conquered world has entered into it. Because you are destitute and unfree, and because you live only halfway, you are destined to say no more often than yes. Your poet cannot do otherwise. You will not read about the glory of the city but about its tears. For the vale of tears is yours. The revolutionary song will exhort you because struggle is your tool. This book is about class and you are its contents. New York, roaring with its magnitude, the business enterprise before you is monstrous and hostile. Well then, may it no longer exist! New, new, new is the star of communism. Its communal labor is creating a new style and beyond it there is no modernity.

U.S. Devětsil

Introductory Poem

Angular image of suffering
is the city
and the great event itself before your eyes,
reader,
you are opening a book unobtrusive and plain
and the song begins.

With its fame
the city has not vanquished me,
its majesty and magnitude have not enchanted me,
I love stars, woods, springs, meadows, and flowers
and I will return into their mysterious embrace,
yet as long as any one of my brothers suffers,
I will not be happy,
and inflamed by the injustice of the world
ceaselessly like now,
leaning against the factory wall, I will choke with the smoke
and sing my song.

And still the street is foreign to me,
it flies like an arrow flung fiercely to conquer the world
and in the rhythm of my blood will never mesh the wheels and
   running belts,
they shackle my hands and the hands of thousands,
so that, when the heart is calling,
companion must not and cannot embrace companion;
yet if I fled into the woods to the deer, flowers, and springs,
such a sadness in my heart would abound,
that without even looking around,
how much beauty, peace, and passion there is,
I would return to town,
to the city, which welcomes man with its iron virtue,
where no nightingale sings and no fir sweetly smells,

where enslaved is not only man,
but flower, bird, horse, and humble dog.

Good reader, you who are reading these lines,
daydream for a while and remember this,
that the angular image of suffering before your eyes
is the city;
indeed like a flower man feels,
don't break don't pick don't step.

Monologue of the Handless Soldier

One day out of the blue
I died in the doctors' arms,
surprised
from a life suffered through
and a sinful lance pierced my heart
and a hand,
their white hand,
deprived my body of its white hands.

For two days in a cold grave I slept,
but on the third
I gloriously rose from the dead,
face like lightning,
vesture like fallen snow,
naked I lay on a pillow
and the sun,
the sun overhead
was my halo;
like a god's my eyes were burning,
but inside of me,
but inside of me on a day unblessed
nevertheless died
two good hands of my body.

The lady who stood next to me
bore sadness in her eyes
and as if she loved me,
she smiled at me compassionately,
but I told her seriously:
dame,
two hands the Lord gave,
two hands the Lord took,
praised be His name.

Never did I curse fate,
endure I did a lot,
with God's grace I will endure this too,
Lose sleep over it I will not.

Only once in a while, when past me went
a wench waiting to be embraced,
my eye with tears glazed
and you hands,
you good hands,
right,
left,
I craved.

Until one day,
I don't know when, it was a strike perhaps,
people took to the streets again.

Treasures,
behind which the heart closed shut,
I think, they did not desire then,
they only wanted to lament to God and people
how the hand with rings is choking them
and commits abuse,
they only wanted to lament their misfortune,
——when suddenly sixty police officers
invaded their ranks.

They told them to the face that it is not human
nor democratic
and that they should be ashamed
to beat up people just like that.
The pavement is hard, will it bear
this injustice?

[7

Why be surprised,
that then with anger, with excitement
they threw stones at them.

Then for the first time I did commiserate,
my hands, my dear hands,
that you were taken once,
once,
by a fiery grenade.

December 1920

In jail,
where you wait for the sun to no avail,
is a table
and it is as poor as a flower bed devoid of flowers,
sad like a cage after the bird flew away;
only a loaf of bread on it shines like the sun
and a cup is sipping sadness.

On this table they sowed the seed of pain,
that in their hearts they no longer could contain
and from it a flower, like a lily, grew,
but it had a red blossom,
which was as sad as human misery
and beautiful like the world.

Near this blossom
a white dove alighted one morn,
and revealed to the whole wide world
that it was Josef Kulda's soul
and came right from the hospital;
how sweet wine is, when you drink it,
so bitter is life, when you live it,
but still that it is a beautiful thing,
that it is a palm filled with sweets,
landscape after a rain,
longing for happiness,
that it is the sun, which is bleeding like a wounded deer,
philosophers' stone,
well of joy,
a shepherd's song played on a shawm,
that it is the eyes of a pretty girl,
into which one might gaze
and the heart bursts into song:

only once a year blossoms May,
love only once in life.

This word
flew like a bird into the net of stars
and above the stars
this word was made flesh,
so that it may dwell among us.

The innocent
descended from heaven like a flower's blossom,
came like a perfume into the street,
unrecognized,
he knew his own,
while the human heart clamoring
beat in warning,
that the innocent
came like a perfume into the street,
descended from heaven like a flower's blossom.

Little does it matter that the friend is dead
and that he already smells,
he began to weave a prayer wreath from words and sighs,
to lay on white clouds;
inside his soul he turned his eyes
and in a magical premonition
he gazed at him with a smile
and said:

Josef Kulda, I bid you, rise!

And lo, he rose
and had the sun not shone as if to a dance,
he would have cried,

he rose and walked lightly in the graveyard,
so as not to soak his clothes with dew,
he was like a reverie
and he had a wholly different face,
he was like a groom, unhappy with happiness
and smelled of rosemary.

Prayer on the Sidewalk

I put on my Sunday shoes,
having polished them,
to make them shine like the stars on street pavement
and because I was hungry,
I thought:
perhaps for a gold piece you can buy Baltic herring,
a sixkreutzer worth of bread
and among so many noble feasters you too will be a guest
at the table of the street,
for dinner set and modest.

With a single fish and one slice of bread
sadly I could not have fed thousands.

The butchers' windows shone like altars in church
upon morning mass,
on their steps I would not mind kneeling the longest,
and since even the doorways to shops were like heaven's gates
with signs, with stars,
listen,
the street burst into hosanna on the organ.

I was thinking about my pretty beloved,
how I'm going to come to her at night
and how into her skirts devoutly I'll lay my head,
pity that my hands cannot more tenderly envelop her,
like the slender stalk of white bindweed
the stem of mullein.

But alas,
they say life grants dreams to poets in excess,
no, life never gives you anything free,
into deep misery
turns each my tiniest joy.

Maybe I have a different heart
and different eyes.

When I felt happiest
and a fair-haired woman gazed at me from a window,
a tram struck a small dog,
one of those pretty ones with a pink ribbon,
which it had, so they may find it among thousands like it at first
    glance.
The street fell silent at once,
only somewhere farther away roared an iron shutter in a store
like a wounded lion
and someone cried out terrified;
likely it was the woman, who had been looking at me,
when she beheld blood gushing high.

The poor thing has its body cut in three,
the head completely mashed by the wheels,
and I wept;
I felt like a child standing over a broken doll,
even like a sinner I did penance
and beat my chest,
when from its hot flesh steam rose to the heavens,
yet it was only then that I loved that dog,
when it no longer needed my love.

This happens with people all the same;
in the whirl of the day and everyday din
we pretend
that we don't even know each other,
but if one of us beholds another in a coffin,
he learns
that in reality he quite liked him

and should have smiled at him at least a little while alive,
having failed to shake his hand.

In the midst of life
and yet in the midst of death
you walk,
thinking perhaps of great deeds,
elated with a thought that will save the world,
but before you realize it,
you are rolling in blood under the wheels of trams,
you die like that white doggie
with a pink ribbon.

The guardian angel hardly always flies after you,
perhaps he falls for a bottle of good wine,
for fresh sausage,
for ham,
and you, man, he utterly forgets.

Pensive
I reached the corner of Fruit Market and Celetná
and kneeling down on the sidewalk,
I raised my eyes to the black Madonna,
who is standing here
and over my head she holds her hand,
and I prayed:

Virgin Mary,
since it is necessary that I too die,
don't let me die like that dog,
let me die one fine day on the barricade of the revolution
with a rifle in my hand.

Language of the Crowd

Loving ourselves,
we are a crowd,
having invaded the street,
we are a waterfall of human flesh
and seething passion,
we are wine sparkling in the street's cup,
we are an ocean,
overflowing in space,
we are a crowd,
a hundred thousand heads,
we are two hundred thousand hands,
which passionately pound on God's kingdom's gates,
we are a miracle beyond miracles,
exhilarated ranks,
we will create overnight
the universe.

The street which arches over us
is the Red Sea's waves turned to stone,
which Moses separated with a magical wave of his hand,
for God willed it so,
that his regiments reach the opposite bank
without wetting their feet;
but woe to the ranks of enemies in shiny armor,
they will die in it
when it closes over their heads,
and drowning,
they will curse their pharaoh.

We are a crowd,
we are tiny flames, blazing out of the earth's crater,
which have united
into a vast fire of power and excitement,
we are a cloud,

lightning from cries dinning darkly with thunder,
we are the petard of wrath, which will burst at the decisive
    moment,
we are a crowd,
if we wanted to and spat on the sun,
it would go out.

Children from the Suburb

In the hospital ward,
where nurses dance like dancers
between bottles with a skull and swords
and between flames of distress,
we stood half naked and pale like chalk
we boys from the suburb,
for vanquished we all are and on the chests of all it kneels
suburban wretchedness.
The windows spoke to us in a strange, obscure speech
of happiness.

A doctor came to us with dark glasses,
under which smiles were erased,
(those were glasses of dissemblance,
perhaps also a bad omen)
his hands shook under the burden of our stares
and he was sad.

Yet when he lay his hands on us
so gently and lovingly,
indeed he seemed so wise to me,
like Maestro Lantner, maker of violins,
and we were violins made from maple wood,
each of us played
some merry or sad song from his life.

For a while he listened to us,
but when he realized that none of these songs was played right
and that all of us are faulty or out of tune,
he sounded us all carefully,
played the ribs' strings quietly
and sang:
e—a—d—g
g—d—a—e

You know, boys,
you all must get well once more,
so that when in the world's streets that great concert will be,
you all can play from a red score
the revolutionary symphony!

And, I say, what a symphony it will be!

At the War Cemetery

Violets bloom in the spring,
Heather blooms in the autumn,
but memories,
deep in the heart sown,
blossomed today inside me,
when the path between graves I walked
leading forth my beloved
with a pink scarf, with a white daisy.

I was thinking:
What if all those who are lying here
burdened the heavens with their prayers
for a little love and for grace,
surely the weight of prayer heaven would break,
snuffed out,
the sun would tumble,
stars falling would shake
and turn dark,
the moon would lose its light;
to earth it would all fall
between houses, onto streets, on grass between flowers
for the love of those who loved
and for the sin of those who had sinned.

Luckily they all remained silent
and fell,
to die,
and then when the bayonet still warm
from their hands was torn,
to be carried by a second, third, and fourth,
again quietly they would lie,
my beloved picked the daisy's petals,
saying: he loves me, he loves me not,
but I mused,

what may mean
that statue stern and stony,
and as if saying litany to all the saints,
I read the names of the dead written in golden print,
invoking them in heaven
on our behalf to plead,
when we will need
strength.

Don't I know that one day great wonders will come
and all the dead here from the dead will rise:
Raguz Stojan,
Tadeus Dyák,
Passereau Charles,
Fedregolli Silvio,
Čechonovič Jefim Semjonovič,
Kazsakar Georg,
Pokorný František
and they all, all of them all around,
when the angel calls from the sky
eye to eye they will stand,
but instead of seeking, for a deadly strike,
the heart under the other man's coat,
they will all embrace,
plant a kiss on the face
and will shake hands as friends.

Revolution

Ardent
in the midst of life we stand
like Wilde before his judges,
gentlemen,
ladies,
misses,
as if with our hand
we wanted to break
the day,
before it crushes us with eyes of amazement.

To the tender mercies
we are throwing our bodies in your midst
and a glassy smile will wedge itself into our eyes,
in threes,
in fours,
in fives
as we stand in our shop windows,
we teach suffering,
and sowing
our beauty with motionless fingers
on street pavement,
we are weaving,
we dye with blood,
we sew banners in red,
the skies, houses, and flowers we tell
that the revolution will come
tomorrow perhaps.

The banner
like the sky swollen with wind
one of us will unfurl,
a standard,

an outcry on a pole,
will scream into people's windows:

hence we,
if you living will not

and gentlemen with shiny top hats
and ladies
dressed for balls,
from hairdressers' windows sad manikins
with beautiful hairdos
united in solid ranks
we will man barricades.

Machine guns
no one will stop crashing worlds
and if thousands of soldiers they send for us,
us against them
will stand up waxen-faced.

The sun
like a bugle in battle will blow into silence,
across dead bodies
and under banners
we will run forward to meet bayonets,
until the river running dry
will billow with blood
when we throw open the gates.

All at once
into the world to the four winds
radios and telegrams will fly,

and tomorrow the whole world in newspapers will read
that in Prague window manikins
hoisted the red flag above the town.

Then only will come those who had been afraid
and not even with force dared withstand,
then only will people come with shame to take
the great victory,
victory,
victory
from our wooden hands.

Good Tidings

For Ivan Olbracht

On alms of manna falling from the sky
into our hungry palms
no future race must anymore have to rely;
from hundreds of tasks which await them today,
we will mostly implant in their hearts you,
revolution,
eternal, growing by the second
like a seed well-watered by dew.

Lo, from distant voyages
explorers are just returning,
carrying on a crowbar in their hands
an enormous bunch of red grapes,
fecund,
sweet
like a day dangling from the sky,
and good tidings,
that in the east lies a beautiful land,
which bears justice.

Farewell to you, our land, native land,
it is not we who are not worthy of you,
rather it is you who deserves us not,
there in the east eyes see salvation,
there in the east, in the cornflower-blue distance,
rises a wreath made from ears of rye,
hammer and sickle.

And the file of the grateful already sets out,
old men, children, men and women,
happiness unending on their faces
their yearning gazes they fasten
where the sun rises;

a chorus of angels fluttering their wings above
accompanies their longing with song:
Glory,
glory to God in the highest
and to his people on earth
revolution.

The End of War

On the forehead bearing fiery signs,
over the body wounds which will fester,
from the whole world to us the wounded came,
some of whom did not want to, did not want to,
yet die they did
as soon as tomorrow or the day after tomorrow,
and others lived despite death, despite wounds and pain,
like living torches of sorrow.

On the way from the station
their sweethearts awaited them like a vernal avenue,
whose boughs almost topple over
with joy over their return and with the mirth of youth;
their mouths were red like a bough's crimson bloom,
for whose touch greedy lips pined
and when they shed petals in rays of hot gloom
on them fruit was ripening, which an eager hand yearned to
    pick.

Under their smiles turmoil turned into sweet dreaming,
across the banks of lips love was oozing softly
and gray days became holidays suddenly.
And their wombs were like the surface of Jerusalem's lake,
which, quietly lying in the sun, still,
waited for the angel to fly down from heaven, to stir it
with the touch of an amorous quill.
Blessed, who believed that marvel
as related by the old legend
in the Gospel of St. John, in the fifth chapter,
to wit that he instantly recovers
who first hurls himself deep into holy water.

The hapless ones dreamed of their happiness
in deep sorrow, in their ponderous grief,
and dove ardently into the still waves of a woman's lap
arms flung open,
so that at least a good woman be their fate,
now that fate was not a good woman to them.

A Chanted Prayer

Brought low by a crown of thorns
from God to man,
breaking, he gave away his beautiful dream
and now he is waiting
for it to be fulfilled.

When human hearts are filled
with his love till they overflow
and in the meantime revolution
cruel,
fair
into palms deals out to each,
poor and rich
the same share.

Oh Lord, leave us, behold, it is getting late.

In the name of love we do not forgive
sins committed,
in the name of love we harshly avenge
lives of the hungry
and wrongs
which man, created in your image,
did unto his brother
on earth,
in heaven,
on sea.

Yet the poet he is still in turmoil:
Lord,
as they tormented you with unmanly pain,
having wreathed you a thorny crown of rose coil,
why wouldn't they at least allow those roses to remain!

Evening on the Porch

I

The evening usually is still like a frozen waterfall,
but the porch it is the embrace of the Virgin Mary,
those who from the battlefield of the day carry away their
    wounded bodies
will seat themselves on it nightly
and it will clasp them with bars like a woman with fingers
    would embrace them lightly;
the sky is full of stars
and under the stars for all wounds, for all wounds there is balm.

Acacias above the tracks ring with scents like the belfry on the
    village green,
to rouse men and women from their sins,
but lovers entwined their bodies passionately and severely,
and so it seemed that on the hillside many entwined hands were
    praying
silently and devotedly,
that the angel brought tidings of love
to an amazed Virgin Mary.

Pity, now that the porch was that fortunate saint,
that those whom she sheltered have long, long been crucified.

II

    Clank!
It was once,
    as if someone had thrown a stone into the window.
The night was sweet,
    as if a bell had begun to sway in your infatuated heart
    and the thick black spider's web of silence

was pierced by song,
which invades the universe like water a crack in a ship on the
sea.

It was the landlord's daughter playing a piano tune,
that little blonde with eyes of blue,
whom I daily humbly implore to love me
and to whom my soul bends its knee.

Hey!
It was a merry tune, it was a tempestuous tune,
one that in the Whale bar a mariner choir may croon.
I quickly thought about her maiden body,
her tender frame composed of rosy bones,
on which pliant flesh trembled with the tide of joy;
I quickly thought about her simple gaze,
which she fixed on the music like on a lover's eyes
and love,
great love soared inside of me from toe to head
like sap inside a white birch tree on a spring eve,
that tree at night has not a single leaf and the shoot swishes in
the wind,
but at dawn it has come to leaf, unrivaled in the world by any
book
and on each a poem.

It's a pity that already four officers visit that miss,
one of whom will take her for a wife and with life's distress
appease;
pity, I would have had her like a garden in front in whose soil
roses, reseda, bluebells, melissa would flower,
and whose gravel paths at night my fingers would travel.

She played,
while our hearts, those indomitable hammers pounding the
    world's treasure-filled vault,
grew silent altogether
and the universe was no longer that ship, invaded by song like
    water,
it was more a glass, filled to the brim with beauty,
and we drank from it to the bottom, to the bottom deeply,
until the head tilted back and a tear entered the eye;
after all it is beauty we need, like love, bread, and water,
so that filled with it we may do everything beautifully,
so that a lover may utter beautiful words to his beloved
and poets write their poems.

Hunger, pain, anguish, grief, anger, and love
left us like birds, when summer lengthens its shadow
and we being,
at that moment we only were,
we were like a stone is, a tree or a flower on a green meadow,
nothing more, nothing more;
where was that city, those streets, those cursed factories,
    workshops and machines,
where was that hard bread, water, poor table and rickety chair?
Each of us forgot all his worries,
and falling into the bottomless present with all senses
he was happy,
after all man is happiest when least of his bliss he thinks.

Father often puffed at his pipe and lit matches that died,
being nothing more than an image of human bliss,
on a bough a bird piped in its sleep, perhaps it had a beautiful
    dream

and slumbered on,
and slugs feasting on fragrant flowers were disguised by shadow
and the song alone rushed into the silence like a suicide into the
    depth below,
but we, we the people on the porch with all our heart deplored
    deeply,
when this night allured us so sweetly,
the hillside across with acacias abloom
and the song echoing,
that here under the starry sky
we could not lie until the end of time.

When it was already late and rather likely
that some neighbors next door wished to rest,
once more as if into the grass, as if quickly posies to pick,
into white keys her hands she immersed,
but now,
    damned!
from deep slumber filled with magic we roused resolutely
and clasped hands.

That's why she longed to lull us with that beauty, that beauty
like in the deep forest the wily Šárka that knight
lulled with kisses and horns filled with sweet wine,
this is why,
so that now she could burst severe and blithe
into that song, which patriots intone and misses in national
    garb,
that song, which is bravely sung by would-be legionnaires,
when on the nation's holiday the street cheers them and the
    flags into their mouths fly,
that insolent song, stirring and hollowly pathetic
about high black boots and a saber whetted to cut both ways.

Ho!
From deep slumber filled with magic we roused resolutely
and clasped hands.

Our house is tiny, somewhere on the outskirts of the city,
a godforsaken place where sleepers are awakened by roosters,
yet who would guess how many folk can be cooped up in it,
if they are needy;
next to me lives a blind accordion player,
above me a consumptive seamstress and a limping sailor,
next door a locksmith at the Daněk factory, a lamplighter, and
    an unhappy widow,
in the basement the caretaker couple,
and they all today forgot about the torment from their wounds,
because the evening was fine,
it came, dressed wounds, and having poured oil like a
    Samaritan,
it pleased with sweet words,
but that song snatched away the dressing and the wounds smart
    again,
luckily that pain came in due time, that pain manly deeds will
    incite;
faith and hope arched up in us like bridges across an abyss,
faith by courage is joined
and for this song I devised an ending utterly different and plain:
we too will not die on straw,
we too will die in the field of battle
and when we fall off the horse, the saber too will rattle . . . .

III

The evening usually is still like a frozen waterfall,
but the porch, it is the embrace of the Virgin Mary,
those who from the battlefield of the day carry away their
　　wounded bodies
will seat themselves on it nightly
and it will clasp them with bars like a woman with fingers
　　would embrace them lightly;
the sky is full of stars
and under the stars for all wounds, for all wounds there is balm.

City of Sin

The city,
city of industrialists, plutocrats, and brutal boxers,
city of inventors and engineers,
city of generals, merchants, and patriotic poets
black with sin it overstepped the bounds of God's wrath
and God ranted;
a hundred times he vowed retribution to that town,
rain of brimstone, fire with roaring thunder,
and a hundred times he relented,
for he always recalled that once he had vowed
that for two just men he would spare his town doom
and his word not to keep seemed harsh to the Lord;

for in the vernal park two lovers were roaming
breathing deeply the perfume of hawthorn in full bloom.

The Screen at the Cinema

Impaled by a ray,
a little white cloud slipped down on it
and because it could be sliced like ice cream,
having cut,
with long stares of their eyes people nailed it
onto the wall of the cinema
and so that it would not overflow
like dough on a pastry board swelling severely,
they framed it.

Crucified,
little white cloud on four sides,
how you've insisted upon our eyes,
we all fell in love with you,
saying:
this is beautiful, this is a marvel,
God!

But ah,
you are a sheet too from Procrustes' bed,
dear life, dear life,
when you are lying on it in bloody torment,
aren't you afraid
that they may cut off your legs or hands?

The devout one delights:
Upon my honor, this is a clean altar cover,
from the chalice streams a beautiful dream
and on the patina lie pieces of Christ
for the Eucharist.

However upon you I like most,
men who have iron fists
and women with small, pliant breasts,

I think to myself: screen, hey hooray,
here pass me one that's real
for me to kiss and feel.

You are that handkerchief,
that Veronica passed to Christ at Calvary
and into which, for her, he impressed his portrait;
he thought to himself: with love she may have from me,
at least it will be enshrined in her memory,
God be with you, God with you, my sweet,
God with you, God with you, my Jerusalem.

In the Garden Gethsemane

Between pebbles, bugs, and serpents
shyly my bare foot I set,
on my way in the garden to pray
to my God;
to each man such a moment appears,
his peers mute to his inquiries,
the giddy moment is tolling like a bell
and man unable to depend on fellow man
enters Gethsemane and kneels down ...
I too loved seven beautiful virgins,
who saved up oil for the wedding night,
I too have my dream,
yet today wearied by life
I kneel on the grass where saxifrage blooms,
to clasp my hands and say:
Father,
if possible, may your angel fly here,
and if he won't help me drink,
at least may he take this cup away from me;
it is easy for you to rule,
but how can I, I a boy, the smallest of the small,
that cup of joy,
that cup of sacred fervor,
alone drain to the bottom all?

City in Tears

If this world miracles knew
and tears that flow from poor men's eyes
into one great river grew,
these salty tears from cries
would flood streets, squares, factories, banks, and palaces,
and cries and moans, rushing upon the city ceaselessly,
would destroy it, until of it only a wasteland and bare ruins
    remained,
where at night, wandering, a jackal would wail;

if only then a Jeremiah could be found,
to cry over the town deep from his soul.

But man does have a heart and the cruelest heart
knows a sweet moment of forgiveness,
my pain so sad, someone else's the saddest,
and so, town, life's joy and my pain, town,
there is no other remedy,
but for me to forgive you and forget all,
for people have muscles of steel
and ever so profound a faith
that a great day will come when wrongs are righted
and the brimful of their pain
into joy they will turn—
and for this our tomorrow
already I would forgive you all, my town, my street and house,
but that your lookout towers, spires, and chimneys under the
    clouds
have left no room even for the sparrow—
and if I loved you a hundred times more,
that I cannot forgive.

To the wisdom of my heart more eloquently the bird speaks
in the dust of streets
and the aeroplane into the sky may it fly,
be it to Mont Blanc or Mount Everest!

The Creation of the World

The earth will be a place desolate
and sad,
through the sieve of stars a lark into heavens will descend
and its singing incomplete will end,
fumes will put out the sun and obscure stars;
in gardens the frost will set icy blossoms aglow
and nevermore shall we behold the blue sky above us,
never will the linden trees bloom as they did before;
there will be no springs issuing from mountains,
in wires alone little electric currents will flow,
and never will colorful flowers be sweetly redolent,
streets will fill up with poisonous gas,
however still
like God's spirit hovered over valleys,
over houses metamorphosed into steel and sorrow,
over factories, shivering with the din of machines,
the thought of revenge will hover,
until we come,
until with our might one with the vengeful thought we become
and create a new world with an almighty deed.

Only then will a new sun be born,
not that poets' toy, perhaps a golden plate, perhaps a disc set
    ablaze,
yet the sun
from land we shall a sea of azure water separate
and a single banner weave to fly on ships of the five seas,
swords and cannons we shall forge into plowshares,
once more to dig furrows into hallowed soil,
into which we will sow swollen seed,
so that again grain may bud and daily bread we have each,
powder magazines we shall sack, fortresses raze,
and a new cathedral build,
where there would be no gods, nor angels with shiny wings,

where everyone would be God and himself would command
and labor again—this time labor truly holy
will make machines, hammers, and chisels ring
and its song will rumble deeply in every city
like fervent prayer.

On the sixth day
however lovers again will tread silent paths,
and the girl holding flowers in her arms
will weave a colorful wreath of blossoms,
indeed her body will be fragrant like ground broken in March,
which is waiting until living, sweet seed sinks into it;
and before reckoning how many silver stars the Great Bear may
    have,
nourished by the word of love, bewitching and plain,
into the furrow of her body a rare seed is laid,
which will grow.

On the seventh day
a seven-hued rainbow arches across the world,
the loveliness of May lilies fills the breast,
having conceived, the beloved spent by the newness of things
will rest.

The seventh day be a holy day.
May the machine grow silent, the hammer be still,
may all violins reverberate and may the flute trill
its soft song.
The seventh day be a holy day.
And a holy day it will be from this day until the end of the
    world.

In a Small Suburban Street

It begins in the middle of town and leads far into suburban
     fields,
winding in a very roundabout way,
those living in it, I trust, in thousands do not count their money;
at night a walker is almost a miracle
and if he strolls, then from the acacias, suffering near walls
     facing the dark factory,
shadows fall on their backs humbly under his feet.

At night the factory lies on a bier like Jairus's daughter,
the mourning blanket of night her form shrouds
and though my steps rumble like the knell's thunder
and though the crow sings a funeral tune beneath the clouds,
dead she is not, is not,
          but is sleeping.

This deathly silence collapses unto itself at the crack of dawn,
when the sirens resound and idle wheels begin to turn,
until from this din the factory awakens to her everyday living.

And when I passed by, I was searching for vicious words and
     blasphemy
with which to humiliate this her majesty,
to strike the pen out of the hands of the poet, who today still
     wanted to create
for this image of civilization and capital

          a servile accolade.

The air oozing steel here saps the strength of the living
and driving belts tear off human limbs with thoughtless force,
as if in the meadow they were merely chrysanthemums to pick,
only so that the machine may feed on tepid blood;

lo, how the pressure gauges preen, appraising strength, lo, how
   the cylinders gleam,
lo, how high the smokestacks stretch, as if they were gun
   carriages,
the muzzle trained at the stars, they are preparing for great wars
in which vain man even the cosmos would like to vanquish.

And when I stood before her, suddenly to me would whisper
from a small window of a cottage, which seemed even smaller,
   sounds in the sweetening dusk,
it was a lullaby and it gently soothed
my aching soul:

> rock-a-bye, rock-a-bye.

and I felt the power of these sounds, not only did they conquer
   silence,
but they also humbled the beauty of the factory, proudly
   looming dark,
those sounds splashing like ocean waves, tall walls could not
   withstand,
under their weight the entire factory trembled,
over all reigned victorious with its might:

> rock-a-bye, rock-a-bye.

At that moment I knew the uselessness of a curse and I was just,
after all that factory itself curses and itself indicts,
   amidst thousands of hearts.
May she here remain, may she loom tall with her stacks in the
   clouds,
indeed for the bliss of the needy, for the bliss of the whole world
   she is quite unnecessary.

A Poem Full of Courage and Faith

I know
you are playful and gentle,
affectionate of heart,
I know
where your glory lies,
the glory of your life,
in your time you want to have, don't you,
humble quiet and humble peace.

You wish for a kitchen, tiny, quite small,
white and silent like a dove sailing above,
on the wall brass pots in whose glaze
at yourself, your youth, and beauty you would gaze,
in the windows curtains of pink lace
and in the flowerpot a blossom,
which shyly became fragrant at dawn
and was sweetly redolent until nightfall;
this would be your kingdom full of smiles,
wouldn't it,
this would be the world attained for which you pray,
still
like a Sunday on the village green at the break of day,
plain
like those twenty years of your life;
there would be so much glory,
wouldn't there,
when in an ardent beat
the mortar would toll in your hand like a belfry's bell,
as you crushed sugar, cinnamon, and poppy seed,
while in the morning breeze
beneath the window on a bough a bird trilled
its melody.

Yet I,
the son of a tempestuous time,
perhaps man, perhaps boy, perhaps child,
in the torrent of events I steep my hands,
day by day tumbling forth;
I am like vernal wind across the lands,
when a blue sky arches to span the world,
when lilacs silently bloom and ice bursts on streams,
I am like vernal wind, which, sweeping the world,
stood in wonder
over the first flower of spring;
and that was you, that was my love
for you.

But today I brace my elbow in vain against fate,
nothing anymore will save me,
because a dream, a great dream tempts my weak heart
with its glory;
I stand on the palm of Europe, where millions crowd,
awaiting the day
when the signal will resound,
when the first blood on the decisive day stains cobblestones,
when the first wounded fall,
on the barricade, on the barricade with my song I shall stand
one of the crowd.

I know
you are playful and gentle,
affectionate of heart,
God's maiden, who meekly yields
to my embrace,
but I,
no, I don't want, I don't want you,
farewell, but you don't need to be sad,
behold, lilies bloom and roses and daisies,
farewell
and visit me one day, when I die.

Poor

I have a window,
in it float spring skies
like a small ship on a river with a pink flag,
I have a dog,
he has human eyes,
I have a blue notebook
and on its pages
thirty-three lovely girls' names,
I have a sharp pocketknife and a pistol,
in my tie a ruby pin,
I have a love who dances on the spring lawn
(at night we go by the graveyard into the fields,
and since she is a hairdresser
her hands, face, and hair are fragrant,
as if not in a featherbed but in a bouquet of roses she had lain
    yesterday)
and so that I don't forget,
I have an empty box of polish,
a sad, bone-dry flowerpot in the window,
a flower on my coat,
and tears in my soul.

When I'm home,
I don't have to watch the street always
at the stars too I gaze,
a comb I play
and I chant,
my fingers drum on the oak table apace
and it feels like someone's embrace.

Clearly someone is going to say:
this for me would not suffice by my faith,
and if it is enough for you,
It would not be enough for me,——

oh, yes, I too would surely be glad
if more I had,
yet I am a wise pauper:
for I am learning from the orbits of the stars
and believe
in the communist manifesto,
I believe that the day will arrive
when I too will be content,
I believe
that I too will one day be master
and high, high, high above Prague
I will fly in an aeroplane.

The Humblest of Poems

On a mountain high and inclining toward the city
standing
hands wide open,
I am a prophet who is leading the way
and augurs the poor their glorious future day,
I am a sage
who advises in times of hopeless pain,
holding in my hand a blossom that will never fade,
I am the one who in the revolution will fire first,
but I am also the one who will be first to fall
and who will be first to kneel to dress wounds of the wounded,
miraculous like God
and mighty like God,
I am more,
I am still much more
and yet I am nothing,
but, humbly resigned to the mercy of multitudes,
the poet
Jaroslav Seifert.

Sheer Love

1923

Electric Lyre

The stillness of the forest with blue skies,
when calyxes close under the weight of darkness
like at night weary human eyes,
the bubbling spring which through green grass
in its surface bears a reflection of stars,
this magic my youth never knew.

Before I begin to sing in a frantic rush
about things that are and that I adore,
through the din of cars, bells, chimes, and wires,
before I begin to sing of the beauty of propellers,
advancing in the supple caress of clouds with force,
and thrusting the eagle, about to fly higher, back below,
about the machine's iron that burns with a luminous glow,
about the power of the crowd, which marches and annihilates,
and about my heart—like an autumn leaf
it flutters in the wind of daily events,
burning with love's flame, which is pink and clean;

before I begin to sing in this everyday din,
to you, Muse, I turn as it is ancient use,
come to me today and kindly shake my hand;

Muse, my modern Muse of our time,
who with a shy motion at night at eight unveils
the red curtain on the white screen of the cinema,
come to me today, the creative hour is arduous;

Muse, you who soars in amazing haste
over the helmet of the cyclist, who at forceful pace
sweeps boldly along the stadium's track.

Muse, you who guides the hand of the engineer,
as he draws a blueprint of an American skyscraper,
come to me today, waning is my vigor
and I take hold of my pen with fear;

proscribed Muse of the street,
you who witnessed when on the canvas of the circus
were painted beautiful pictures
in which a black man resists a tiger's clutches;

Muse, you who hovers over the head of the lion tamer,
when he cracks the whip and curbs fearless predators;

Muse, you who holds the hoop for the foolish clown,
for whose jokes the circus roars like the ocean;

Muse, you who knows how tenderly with your hands
to hold the reins to guide the unruly steed
upon whose head a white danseuse stands;

you good Muse, understand my perplexity,
I want to sing out all that stirs humanity
even my love's dream, and that one is sweet;—

the street is my electric lyre,
I walk in its midst, like strings above me are wires,
an iron song I want to intone for the city of stone,
may it be a modern song and today's sacred chorale;

therefore, Muse, come and give me strength,
and so that this song of mine may be fine,
bend your white brow over my lyre.

Poem of Spring

Miss, you sit in the office among typewriters,
the sun of spring brilliant on your fingers
and your hands are shaking, Jesus Christ,
you would surely like to have an airing.

Isn't it true, life is beautiful beyond measure,
the bench in the park may be very hard,
yet people in love write poems with all their heart
and will even that hard wood treasure.

I know, to love is not so easy,
man is tossed back and forth by love's tide,
for a little while he soars up into the sky,
the ray of the sun follows at his side,

yet out of the blue the Earth's relentless weight
strikes him back down
and harsh reality ties him to the ground;

don't worry about it though, fiercely in a while
you will blaze to the stars, falling into an embrace,

for you are young, twenty years old,
and at that stage any merry love is grievous,

because love is like the entire universe:
while it may be bitter, it tastes delicious.

And if you believe me and I can offer you
friendly and true advice,
don't ever be afraid, Miss, to love;

and if someone kisses your right cheek,
turn the left one too.

Amorous Stanzas

Give me your hand, my beloved,
give me both your hands,
I am glad that you delight me so
and that I too delight you,
I may be small and not much that meets the eye,
my love though reaches to the silvery star,
my love is more powerful than all the states in the world,
more terrible than all armies with their cannons' fire,
and its force is beyond compare
with the force of electric engines, and those, if only they desire,
could the universe even with its stars demolish entire.

For love is something enormous;
you can see it for instance in this,
that if the whole world were waging war
and a lot of blood were flowing,
in the sky like crimson angels
fiery shrapnel of steel would fly,
that if the whole world saw revolution,
still somewhere in green grass
lovers would have time to clasp hands
and face to face to incline.

Give me your hand, my beloved,
give me both your hands,
I am no longer afraid that love could play a trick on me
in these revolutionary times,
times when an army of soldiers and hordes of troopers
ready to charge they stand
and millions of poor working stiffs
are preparing for a determined battle,
to show the right of overworked fists
and for that damned toil
earn themselves a little bliss and joy.

If for love I am losing my head and have
nights sleepless and drab,
if all day for love I will sigh
and out-cry my eyes for tears,
don't be afraid, my good friends, that amid this love's blaze
I will forget that which to us is dearest,
that I forget the poor's woe and wretchedness and that love will
    prevent,
that I raise the banner of hopes,
no, not that: love for great things carries away my heart
and if my beloved all so firmly
around her neck would tie my hands
and ever mightily her love to her lap dragged me nether,
to the barricades, to the barricades, when revolution comes,
my beloved and I will go together.

Paris

À Ivan Goll

I no longer feel like strolling along the riverbanks,
when over Prague misty darkness is hovering,
the water is murky, it has no meaning,
it empties into the Elbe somewhere near Mělník;
I no longer delight in roaming
the same streets with nothing new to see,
and in sitting on a bench in the park at night,
where police peek at couples with a flashlight;
here everything is so sad, even things taking place,
life never derails in its trace,
and if something comes to pass, some uprising, strike, or killing,
all will again conspicuously grow chilly.
My sweet, isn't everything here rather silly,
there is no delight for us in this place.

And since it was not granted to me to be born
somewhere on the verge of a dark African jungle,
where the white heat of the sun inflames all into fire
and in the branches auburn monkeys tumble,
since it was not granted to us in the waves of the Nile
to bathe our bodies, looking into the eye of a voracious crocodile,
on the waters to pluck lotus blossoms,
leaping to escape from lion's fangs,
when hungry, to feast on juicy coconuts
and to slumber in the tempest of waterfalls,
since it was not granted that we, natives black and curly,
could to our heart's content bask in the rays of the blazing sun,
why, why did fate mete out to us to live our life
in the streets of this town on the fiftieth parallel line,
where foreign to all is any fierce and fiery swing
and good people breathe with such difficulty,
where all emotion must wither before it even inflames,
where people's necks are encased in stiff starched collars,

where instead of birds we rather listen to jazz bands
and to see lions we go only to the menagerie?

Since it was destined to be and in this stony city
around machines, hammers, and levers hardened soft fists
and iron civilization already means so much to us,
that amidst trees and meadows the city we will miss,
since we are forever bewitched in labyrinths of factories, which
    reek,
why, why did fate mete out to us to live our life just here?

There in the west on the Seine is Paris!

At night, when the skies there light up with silver stars,
on the boulevards stroll crowds amongst numerous cars,
there are cafés, cinemas, restaurants, and modern bars,
life there is jolly, it boils, swirls, and carries away,
there are famous painters, poets, killers, and Apaches,
there new and uncommon things occur,
there are famous detectives and beautiful actresses,
naked danseuses dance in a suburban *varieté*,
and the perfume of their lace with love addles your brain,
for Paris is seductive and people cannot withstand.

Of the local poets I treasure very much Ivan Goll,
for he likes the cinema as well as I,
and believes the saddest of all men to be Charlie Chaplin.

Boxing matches, that too is a nice show,
when man is wistful and sighs for all his devotion,
clank, an eye for an eye, clank, a blow for a blow.

In the sky slowly the Great Wheel is revolving
and when at sunset Paris is already dim with shadow,

lovers are taking walks together along the Trocadéro,
and if earthly dust weighs down their shoes
so that heavenly beauty they may also taste,
to the stars up the Eiffel they fly in an electric lift,
holding one another gently around the waist.

Here everything is so sad, even things taking place,
life never derails in its trace,
and when I fall asleep as night darkens in the window,
I dream that at Père-Lachaise in the thujas the nightingale
    sings.

And, really, Paris is at least one step closer to heavenly spheres,
come, my love, let's go to Paris.

Hour of Peace

A poet's instrument is the lyre,
may it resonate,
when your hands in shackles are encased
by the world of today,
when whirling life, which dins in alleyways,
in the window flashes by,
when cars drive and horns cry,
the factory towering with its black chimneys
and a moment of quiet means great happiness.

A poet's instrument is the lyre,
may it resonate,
a woman wipes a tear from her eye,
lifting a child into her embrace.

There are things in this world that seem,
there are things that are,
hard is the bread that daily we deal
and it grows bitter under a gaze;
comfort the wretched one,
the whole world she held to her fluttering heart
and now that the edges of reality hurt her hands,
now as over her own child she bends
full of burdensome malaise,
of the entire world her tiny, weak infant
is too heavy to bear in her embrace.

Windowpanes and in them green plants
separate the world from her,
they are like sordines on violins;
when the street is droning, the world dashing,
here only hum is heard like that of bees,
and the world, it seems like nothing but flowers
when through this window perceived;

but out there beggars are whimpering prayers of need,
but out there gold is jangling,
and if the stars shone a thousand times more brightly,
in the streets there would be filthy mud,
and if the earth were different a hundred times,
people's souls would always be covered with grime.

Woman, you who weeps over everyday fate,
I implore you, don't you falter,
for you, for you the whole world with my hands I will alter
and this whole sad and ugly globe
I will recast into verse of fine and sweet yearning;
the present barren for love like a stone,
yet when they touch, hands are miraculous,
on the poor table from little bread will grow
and in your heart you will again feel young joy.

A poet's instrument is the lyre,
may it resonate,
and my hands fell into its strings like birds,
there is still beauty that does not decline,
it waters flowers withered in the heat
and where there is beauty there is a soft smile,
and where there is a smile there is tenderness,
and where there is tenderness until the end of time,
loneliness you will not sense.

Listen, softly my fingers play in the strings
a most beautiful melody,
There are things in this world that seem,
there are things that are—

and song, fade away!

Only the last tone may reverberate as if forever
love is dying in memories shyly,
be silent, lyre, poet's instrument:

the baby in its cradle is crying.

Lullaby

Between four walls the ceiling is sagging,
a mother is rocking her little child,
above them the lamp is hovering,
as if an angel to heaven were ascending
and fluttering its wings disturbed moths.
The cradle is rocking from side to side,
the mother's eyes fill with tears
and as if through crystals the baby she sees
and as that cradle is rocking and rocking,
the mother is singing:

—So content sleeping here you lie,
my sweet little child,
and before the stars light up the sky,
your mommy will rock you;
but outside, between tall residences,
in town squares and between palaces,
people are pacing and lamenting,
returning home from work.

—Daddy will come soon.

—So content sleeping here you lie,
my tiny little child,
smiling you cannot divine
why poor people so often moan and cry,
why people each other a slice of bread deny.

—Daddy will come soon.

—When from this doorstep one day
for the world you will leave,
there will be no hunger and no more pain,
this lonely world Garden Eden will be.

The birdies will pick crumbs from your palm,
and since there will be no more cruelty and harm,
from forests hinds and fawns into the streets will come,
the streets will be blithe,
from windows banners will fly,
and people like brothers
will love one another.

—So content sleeping here you lie
under lock and key;
sleep well and slumber, so that you won't hear,
when one day out of the blue
beneath the windows a lovely song will ring,
when all the poor walk by and sing,
—Daddy too will go with them—
when overhead the red banner flies,
shots resound and smoke whirls in the skies
and someone falls with blood in his eyes.
————————————————————————————————
The mother falls silent, the song still softer grows,
dusk gives way to night, a night deep and murky,
lamplighters light lamps with long poles,
slowly the cradle keeps rocking
and as it is swaying and swaying,
the mother softly sings:

—lala, lalalala, lalalala, lala.

New Year's Poem

On the waves of Hamburg's harbor moors a heavy ship,
on the waves your steamer moors, Mr. Hugo Stinnes,
and on top of all the riches that in your coffers you keep,
from America it still brought you a load
of large, heavy, and shiny lumps of gold.
Yet what would you say, wealthiest of men,
if one day I slipped into your abode
at night on tiptoe, so that you would not hear my step,
and if from that robber's pile of your prize
I stole a piece, a tiny glittering nugget,
which would flame like a fragment of the sun the size of a bird's
    egg.

To be sure I would not buy a black horse for it,
though it must be awfully nice to ride along Stromovka,
the horse's hooves stamping the violet's smell and the beauty of
    the bluebell,
and ride up to the summer seat and to the little pond downhill;
when in love, I don't consider myself much,
my dearest, I remember only you,
for if we love, we split our hearts in two,
from the wound opened by kisses power will gush.

Surely it is sad when nearly numb with cold
we stand on Celetná at the furrier's window
and behind glass from the jungle a beast of prey
bares its sharp fangs and its fur heavy and warm,
widely displayed it lazily lounges there prone,
vainly warming the glass case's wooden floor.

So that you don't freeze like a flower in winter,
to prove my love, to prove that you I want to cherish,
for that piece of gold I would have sewn from a rare pelt
a gray little fur coat, with white blotches.

A whole month already I have thought of little else
and in my mind I see how very becoming
the gray little fur coat would be with whitest ermine,
thick and shaggy, so you would be hard to embrace.

What a stir it would create on Wenceslas Square
when I lead you through the flowing queue of people!
Perhaps people would maliciously talk right there,
after all, only pain man will not envy his fellow man.
Surely they would say: Look here, this is a proletarian poet,
since when is poetry today such a lucrative trade?
For so long he wanted bravely to die on the barricade,
until it brought him nice pay;
now that his sweetheart such a precious fur has acquired
and struts around town like her ladyship in a fur coat,
likely he surrendered his revolutionary lyre
and he hardly writes verses about the revolution.

Fools, you may think whatever you like, for all I care,
that perhaps I won the class lottery you may speculate,
or even that writing verse pays off nowadays—
—for you, people humble and abased, for you, my proletariat,
my heart is beating with zeal,
in the first line for you I will always stand,
when the bugle briskly bids to combat,
from you I originate and for you I truly feel,
and so my pockets will always be empty.

Why though shouldn't I for my sweet buy
a little gray fur coat speckled with white,
it is cold, like a tiny bird frost and snow she fears,
for holes in her pockets she cannot tuck in her hands;
a muff which she has worn perhaps five years,
like an old and scruffy dog it is only shedding fur,

when the wind blows, from it in tufts hairs will fly,
even if warmed with her breath her hands are numb.

I would walk on her side in the cold and freeze,
my whole body shivering and chattering teeth,
yet she would always warm me with those hands of hers,
most gently clasping me to her warmth,
my numb nose she would always press to her cheek,
which is fragrant like bitter chocolate,
and she would caress me peck after peck,
until the warmth of love revived me.

Then we could embark on a journey by rail
perhaps as far as the Giant Mountains, to high peaks and to
    valleys,
where the air is full of frosty snowy filaments,
where there is only frost and frost, white snow and silence,
where from the sky frozen birds fall to earth into the snow
and people on skis as if devoid of reason glide down the slope,
where even the bells in belfries are bursting with the frost
and everyone must carry along a flask with a drop of rum.

— —

Farewell, my dreams, you are too radiant and impossible,
on the waves of Hamburg's harbor moors no vessel,
Mr. Stinnes has no heart and his safes are burglar-proof.
At the café window my love and I are sitting together,
in it the frost is painting a tangle of flowers on a misty panel,
so that we may not see the street of the rich—; and here at this table
we shall wait for the first swallow on the aeroplane's wing to
    alight,
until the poet, praising love, writes a poem of spring,
until the vernal wind makes telegraph lines sing,
and lovers once more in groves will stroll,
along the way white May lilies to pick.

A Song about Girls

A long river runs through the town's center,
across it seven bridges reach,
on the embankment stroll a thousand lovely girls,
and different is each.

From heart to heart you wander to warm your hands
amidst rays of love warm and magnificent,
on the embankment stroll a thousand lovely girls,
and none of them is different.

Glorious Day

As it behooves a true proletarian bard,
on the first of May I was on Wenceslas Square,
joining the ranks of carpenters, metalworkers, laborers, and
    cobblers,
among those who have little or nothing at all,
not a penny in the pocket, in the heart woe thousandfold,
and under red banners that were flying passionately,
we vociferously cried out into the blue sky
speeches full of defiance, force, insults, and pride,
the tinkle of gold and tricky talk of socio-patriots
in a roaring storm of cries quickly to drown.

Spirits were high, in the quivering wind
the perfume of bird cherries from some faraway green,
it beckoned to sing a song of spring, full of cheer
about the sun, about love, to honor all amorous couples,
but we in the name of rights and in the name of justice,
did come in order to demonstrate
against that which they burden us with today.
Away with the bourgeoisie, the idol of capital may tumble,
long live Russia, hail to you Third International!

No wars, no swindles, nothing of that kind,
we want a new world, a world to our measure;
for life is lovely and flowers smell sweetly,
the earth is breathing a new, balmy pleasure,
and we the multitude today were hungering for her.
For too long we have toiled for that bourgeois bunch,
for too long we have put ducats into their pockets,
and there was no leisure for us to lounge
in Stromovka, with its fragrant acacias, lilacs, and violets
and precious exotic flowers for bourgeois nostrils,

where in the restaurant busily and merrily all day
waiters will carry mugs of beer to the tables
and an army band clamorous marches will play;
to be sure, in the name of rights and justice
we are fed up, we have had enough of all this,
and he who all his life knows nothing but fast
wishes for once, freed from all misgivings,
calmly to sit down at a bountiful table's repast
and to listen to beautiful sounds of music,
as if it were the quivering of angels' wings.

We citizens unfettered, free, at you, bosses and cowards,
today we thunder into your ears: we want more, we want
     everything,
we too want to dine on pork roast and cabbage,
and for supper to have veal stuffed or fricassee;
we demonstrate and strongly state: may you not forget,
none of you bosses up there,
we too want to drink bottles of burgundy
and eat marinated eel,
and we harbor a firm and indomitable belief
that one day we too will sit down in peace
around tables with wheels of Swiss cheese,
and for all that grief and all that need
from the plenty of the earth's lavish bounty
we too want to choose among the most tasty
smoked salmon, casks of caviar, and salami,
and since we firmly believe in the iron logic of history,
we trust that we too one day will drink liqueurs,
and for the wrongs that we and our forebears endured,
we and our offspring will then ride in automobiles.

For this is what vengeance demands, so it must be,
this is our great dream and strong shield in the field,
and this is why on this glorious day, on the first of May,
hearts filled with anger and yearning, we took to the street.

—————————————————————————————

Beside me with joy, clutching a carnation in my hand,
with my eyes I counted the throng unending and long.

Verses in Remembrance of the Revolution

The autumnal mist in the walls of the street
was swiftly broken by metal files of automobiles,
and red banners, of which there were thousands,
above the heads of the crowd fused into a blazing fire,
and those were not long telescopes on the lookout tower,
nor was there hardly a bearded astronomer,
those were gun carriages of cannons, as Red Guardists sought
to tear down to its foundations the old order,
and on the horizon, on street pavement, and in poor soil,
as well as in the human palm,
they discovered the five-pointed star, which will shine
like the morning star from afar,
it was no dormant volcano that erupted and yet Europe
    trembled,
and rattle did the windows of governments and departments,
it was no lava, which was flowing tepid all about in streams,
it was blood, blood, blood of humans,
to that polyphonic melody we listened with piety,
and fools in those days we did not believe,
thinking that all this was not at all possible,
that it was not force, but that it was a miracle,
and when overnight within reach
a new land suddenly emerged,
we thought it was a mirage.

And when we put our fingers into the wounds today
and the fallow of the earth with human blood dressed,
five times it has yielded crop, five times it was plowed,
it is not a dream, it is not a dream,
witnesses of these deeds we came to be,
and today our hearts stirred with strange sense,
perhaps since the revolutionary breath of those days
blew hotly into our face.

When today this glory, this glory we see
under the blue of the firmament
and when of ourselves we feel ashamed,
that for our weakness only a wonder we wanted to believe,
when we know what was only yesterday,
and know what must happen very soon,
when we know that it is our fate
to sacrifice our blood for the good of the poor,
when we know that the land will be ours tomorrow
and that for our magnificent resolve
this land will be much more lovely,
when we know the delicious moments at night under an apple
    tree,
when the apple tree is blossoming
the May night fragrant with the strong perfume of spring,

when revolution must, must arrive tomorrow,
when we have a sweetheart with hands soft as snow,
when we know all this, I would like to know
why even today we may find some cowardly mate,
who, gazing into a skeleton's hollow,
will meditate: to be or not to be, ah, that is the question.

Verses about Love, Murder, and the Gallows

PROLOGUE

For sheer love I hurried away to the railway,
the stars were veiled by the fumes from the speeding train,
the night was fair, for each night is marvelous,
the world seems just, sleeping under the haze of darkness.

Jičín's town square is most lovely at nighttime.

Smile at me, statue of Mary, from beneath your golden lashes,
in the company of the black shadow I am lonely,
the moon entered the tower window and soon in the dark it
    vanished,
smile at me, statue of Mary, from beneath your golden lashes,
before your fair eye in the quiet of the arcade I pass by.
The tower's tip is like a magnet, swimming in circles across the
    sky,
into the middle of the town square it is drawing emerald stars
and if only one among those thousands suspended above,
plucked loose, fell onto the square from the sky's expanse,
resembling a drop of wine in a delicate cup of glass,
under your feet a vast glow would overflow,
for the star would shatter on the fountain's step of stone
and from profound dark an awfully haunting scene would arise;
it would not be a dream, a phantom, or deluding lies,
but an actual town, stretching below beneath tall peaks
and on the horizon mountains, snow, lakes, and deep ravines,
on the slopes herds of cows and blooming wild roses.

This town I love like none other in the world,
a great deal of my life I pass within its walls,
pity, that there among the roses no joy for me will thrive
and that journeys there drank from my tears, hearing my sigh.

If in town the majority fell to communist comrades,
I would request from the famous council of the city
when I die surely a monument for me to raise
somewhere at the end of Linden Tree Avenue near Libosad;
on a tall pedestal of white marble
legs astride I would stand lyre in hand,
so that I could gaze at the town and the stars overhead.

The Linden Tree Avenue, surely the world's one and matchless,
where nightly all the town's pretty girls will wander,
and I would glance into the eyes of every lass
with a gaze welling forth from a heart of ardor.
That perhaps would be bliss vast and unceasing,
to be in love with all girls right and left,
to love all girls and have a heart of stone and undying,
to love all the girls and never to be misled.

Frozen in a moved gesture I would stand above the linden trees,
heavily fragrant the linden trees would din with the buzz of
    bees
and for the lovers, dazed with that perfume and their love,
amidst amorous whispers and kisses a song of love I would sing:
that to love someone is not facile and effortless,
softly the lyre would ring: strum, strum, strum, strum,
the sad ballad about a hapless tailor I would narrate,
who also loved and who in the end by the hangman
with his hempen noose was stripped of his love's dream.
For none of those who are strolling here today
has yet seen how fearfully grave a thing love can be.
Each is merry and merry, joyfully their love's dream they
    dream,
yet you, my lyre, into their amorous whisper you would thrum
about unhappy love a sad and mournful tune:
strum, strum, strum, strum.

BALLAD

Just as a cloud is pierced by the spire of a tower,
so was the quiet love of Jan Trnka, tailor in Jičín,
he loved his wife, for in any woman's embrace
we always conjure up life's fairest fantasy.
Over a low cradle, which like a calm heave
lapped against the chamber wall, the woman leaned
and the tailor sewed, fond words to the machine's beat
in harmony fused when they echoed in her melody.
And in the nook four children head to head would sleep,
to them belonged mother's smile, which she shared,
giving half to her mate, whom she loved dearly,
half to her brood, whose fate night and day she'd await.

So time passed and with time years amassed
over the family's happiness, living in plain silence,
apart from the current of events, away from the world.

Yet the devil never sleeps; the temptation of sin
on his wing is sweet-tasting,
you extend your hand hesitating and that instant
woman's embrace engulfs you and your lip to a lip clings,
as if soon you were to perish and so in haste
the sweetness of her breath you wished to taste.

Why only did you come, you, the soap boiler's fair child,
from blue woolen fabric to have a dress made,
you knew your beauty's temptation and that the tailor would
    not withstand,
you knew that your body is a marvel delicious with sin,
that your breasts are like grapes while the mother's chest
has withered, her beauty she gave to her children indeed
like honey the flower with its fragrant blossom gives the bee,

you knew that when the tailor took your measure
and when over your white frame he bent,
your body he would touch with his hand
and your bosom's buds he would long smell.

The willfulness of fate toyed with the poor tailor laughably,
once sitting from dawn till dusk, he sewed with ceaseless industry,
yet since into that fair maiden's eyes he has gazed,
with all devils the wretched tailor is possessed;
he is sad like a child and when he wields his needle
from his window he watches the square sighing quietly.
The statue of the Virgin Mary is smiling at the blue sky,
to her he raises his eye ever so hesitant and shy,
the bitterest lot in the world is the lot of love,
at mournful lovers the lovely Virgin does not smile.

Then came long nights filled with grief and tears,
her own suffering felled the pitiful wife,
the cradle has stood still and the tiny child weeps,
yet mother has no words of solace for it;
only hot tears drip from her eyes onto white lace,
dusk has arrived, ajar into the night the window is silent,
thirteen tinny stars glisten above the blessed Virgin,
at the café Paris they are playing a weepy song,
bent over her own pain the woman is crying and sighing.

The moon and stars rise in the clouds, it is now
that lovers vow to love till death may them part
and the two who cuddle strolling are a couple exceedingly
    comely,
dazed is the tailor by the gaze into her dark eyes,
the moon gleams in them and he is walking in his sleep
and on the wings of passion he rises into giddy heights of the
    night;

for his passion he forgets his wife's bitter tears,
he begins to dream new dreams on his lover's bosom,
he is like a butterfly in the calyx of a pretty blossom,
and that which he sees in one sole gaze from her eyes
no poet in the world in words could cast.

In the star-filled night, high above Jičín,
Zebín is flowering pink, in the dark a bird his nest is seeking,
lovers walk the avenue alone hand in hand in the shade,
the best pillow is the green meadow smelling of cumin,
when no one any better will provide.

First the wife cried, now with her five children weep,
first with tears she reproached and now she nags him with
    words,
into his sweet infatuation she blends bitter venom,
her weeping is like an owl's nocturnal song.

—What have you done, tailor Trnka, known across town,
grave, the gravest is your trespass, irremissible sin,
moon cease your light and you stars, awe him with dark,
when at night he will wander somewhere in the park.

For a bit of love the tailor suffers all with resolve,
for a bit of love he endures any woe,
only the children he pities, when his eye rests on that,
he feels so anguished that tears he wants to shed.

And already people in town are talking, shouldn't he be
    ashamed
and what a disgrace around town scandal to create,
yet his heart trembling with the beat of nightly kisses
the tailor returns at the cock's crow mornings late
in his dream at dawn his hands implore her shadow.

The smallest child in white downs calmly sleeps,
it hears not how his lover by sweet names he calls in his dreams
and the rest of them scared at their father stare
when delirious, while mother with eyes ablaze,
at the window, in her palms holds her teary face
and with a white handkerchief tear by tear will erase.

In the end Trnka came to see that it could not go on like this
and the weight of fate on him heavily came to rest,
life was nothing to him but a string of painful suffering
and love only a brief flash of bliss awfully scarce.

This was no longer that first hard blow of a heady wave,
he would muse with the clock, glumly striking on the spire,
yet in his lover's arms his dread he could no more escape,
when in his tangle of feelings he felt utterly mired;
and reeling between two women day after day,
he saw that someone else rolled the dice for his bliss,
who will finally arrive and grimly proclaim:
punishment for trespass or for love the sweetheart's kiss;
yet no one was coming and the tailor in his thoughts would
    surmise
that we ourselves each our good fortune devise:
—Either my neck I break, then comfort, Lord, my widow,
or the wife passes away—and on her grave
green myrtle will sprout, which into your hair I will braid
when I take you across the square as my bride in white
while the trumpets, violins, and clarinets sweetly play.

Devilish temptation fuels the tailor's force
and in his mind he is painting his deadly design,
in his mind around her white neck he lays the noose,
for the price of her death he will know happiness,
he will kill his wife, hang her,

and the people will say: dear soul, the awful pain she couldn't
    bear,
took her own life, the good unfortunate woman,
the tailor is a villain, may he one day find
what it means to love and not to be loved.

That day, when in him this decision came to fruition,
everything turned into things beautiful and kind:
the flowers fragrant and the wind forces legs to dance,
pity that each day floats away with the evening cloud.

— —

In the gas lantern, which illuminated street corners,
the white mantle slipped down and gas burned scarlet,
along the mast the light was oozing down, as if it were blood,
onto the cobblestones of sidewalks into crimson pools.
The last drunks carried it on the soles of their shoes
into homes, where their wives were still awake,
and those traces glowed red in the dark and bloody,
as if someone had killed, as if a murder had occurred,
the pond's nocturnal surface quietly entered windows,
under downs sleepers were dreaming their small-town dream,
but one window was wide open,
from the dark a colored image appeared, like on the cinema
    screen,
over the cradle a woman leaning and a man inclined to the
    woman,
he holds her hands and gazes at her kindly:
Don't cry, woman, I surely love you, don't cry,
for my children my life I would give, for they are mine,
and the woman with tears in her eyes must smile
and into the tailor's eyes too peer warmly;
rising from the cradle, she hesitates shyly,
and she lovingly clings to her husband,

nervous the tailor fingers in his pocket
the hempen noose with his hand.

Don't cry—woman—I surely love you, don't cry,
he was overcome by a strange compassion for his wife,
but gaining control the word of love he in her throat tightened
    with a noose
and her eyes, those eyes, that wanted so much still to smile,
they stared at him bulging terribly all this while;
air only she grasped when she groped for his hand
and the tailor, scared, the noose quickly pulled tight,
with her hand she braced herself and then she fell hard,
rolling down on the ground beneath the cradle.

Then his hat he took and left. Bulging eyes
after him are turning with a ghastly stare,
as they had watched tearfully when he walked away,
the town square was silent, but humming was the tailor's head,
as if columns of soldiers he faced
and ten drummers would just then drum
a muffled march: da da da da dum dum dum,
yet all was quiet and the tailor was alone,
towering in mid-square was only a statue of stone,
thirteen tinny stars were shining in her eyes.

It was night and the stars then were curiously lovely,
above the tip of the spire the moon stood still
and the tailor on the step to the stony fountain
in a broken voice to the empty silence complained:

For sheer love I begot children five,
for sheer love I had to take another life.
Five orphans are weeping and so sad I am,
folks, folks, do not damn me or condemn.

For sheer love I begot children five,
for sheer love I had to take another life,
in the linden trees my love is waiting and it feels so sweet,
folks, folks, do not damn me!

But a black cross on the table stands and a candle burns
and love things the judges in robes do not understand,
rheumatism plagues them and their faces are wan,
they speak of love, passion, and kisses, yet an eyelid they will
    not bat.
For tears the tailor cannot see outside into the land
and he feels sad because he knows that had he planted myrtle
    on the grave,
someone else perhaps may have plucked it today.

The world's saddest place is the prison courtyard,
a flower does not bloom there, nor the sun shine,
but a song is heard soft and low from afar,
the clock striking at times shatters the silence,
in a hempen noose the tailor Trnka now does hang
poor wretch, not even a snow-white lily in his hand.

EPILOGUE

It is spring again, soaring to the stars, the bird sings,
and it sings near midnight late, as it used to sing last year,
again it's a night of spring and Zebín is flowering pink,
to their beloved's blouses, fragrant with bunches of violets,
yearning the lovers once more trustingly lean,
each is merry and merry, joyfully their love's dream they dream
in vain the lyre sang: strum, strum, strum,
about unhappy love a sad and mournful tune;

lovers rather listen to the nightingale's song, which is not the
    same,
with its pain thus it fulfills relentless fate,
for where flowers in the fall were burned by frost and the cold,
in the spring again new blossoms will grow.

A Sailor

On the seashore a lighthouse is burning into the night,
eleven sailors are shooting craps at the bar named Whale
and drinking grog from steaming cups;
the twelfth sailor is not there.

The twelfth sailor is wearing a blue cap
and a shiny black mustache, truly becoming him,
he is roaming the harbor in a colorful throng,
blowing smoke from his pipe to the yellow moon.

For this sailor from the vessel *Olympic*,
wearing a shiny mustache and a blue cap,
the perils of love he scorns with mirth,
and rather than shooting craps at the bar named Whale,
he chooses to leave the round of eleven
and roams the dockside street.

He knows full well that this very evening,
among the girls, thousands of whom here he will see,
may at least one be
who will surely greatly fancy
his black mustache and blue cap,
so it is better to wander the narrow port alleys
than to shoot craps at the bar named Whale.

The twelfth sailor is awfully strong
and his heart is bold,
on this globe there are five continents
and on each continent many a port,
one of them is always the most magnificent;
and on his voyage around the world
the sailor his mustache will twirl,
in agreement with the captain
the *Olympic* in one of them will land.

And he found for himself one beauty in each,
who fancied his mustache
and to whom he vowed his brief love;
in agreement with the captain
the *Olympic* will always dock there
and the sailors go ashore.

Yet rather than sit in the bar named Whale
with his eleven mates,
he is missing from their round,
and with his cap and twirled mustache
he is wandering on the shore late at night,
until far on the sea open and wide
in inky waves the rays would shine.

And when he goes aboard again,
he never mourns;
he knows that in two short months,
among the thousand girls who are in the port,
he will seek the eyes of his second love
by the yellow light of the moon.

When the second one too sees him off in tears
and far away from her he sails,
sitting on the deck of the ship under steam,
his third sweetheart gladly he anticipates.
And this one is black as night and her eyes
are two stars that at night would gleam.

The fourth sweetheart lives in an Eastern land
and she also loves his mustache and his cap,
when they part she carries chrysanthemums at her heart
and from her slanted eyes tears stream down her face;
but there is no time for this grief,

the ship's funnel gushes forth wreaths of smoke,
the captain is standing on the bridge
and the vessel sails onto the rippling sea.

And roaming on his voyage around the world,
to the fifth continent he sails,
the sailor pleased, his mustache he twirls
and sits on deck in the shade.

When with the fifth sweetheart too he parts,
deep night has fallen at sea,
the ship's funnel gushes forth smoke in wreaths;
only then does the sailor know grief,
for on the shore no lighthouse beams,
and moved at the stars he gazes in the sky.

To him it seems that in the constellation of fair Cassiopeia,
which looks like this:

his five sweethearts sadly at him smile;
five stars, five tear-stained faces,
five smiles, moving one to tears,
in the constellation five stars above the sailor shine,
his sweethearts about him reminisce;
on each star he sees a teary cheek,
onto bosoms that are red, black, yellow, brown, white
silently tear after tear drips,
sweethearts in Australia, Asia, Europe, Africa, and America
are weeping for their mariner.

Yet the ship on its voyage around the world
again is approaching the first port,
merrily the sailor again his mustache he twirls,
and rather than shoot craps in the bar named Whale
when the ship docks there,
he chooses to leave the round of eleven.

A Black Man

A fresh breeze blows on the ocean's shores
and between empty conches and pieces of washed-out coral
content black women prostrate they lie,
while the waves of the high tide slowly rise;
I believe it is a sad lot to be nothing but a European,
to this fate myself I cannot resign,
God, if only to sit in the shade of palms,
or like those black women on the shore to lie.

And this black boy bids farewell to us today;
forgive me, Master John, you I must envy,
twelve days from now on the shore with black women you will
    play,
    the train is beginning to leave,
    the ship is sailing
    and the aeroplane flies above the sea
and I sitting in the train station's restaurant,
over civilization's beauty silently I cry,
what use are aeroplanes, those metal birds, to me
when in them I cannot fly,
and in clouds above me into the distance they fade.

    Oh, Master John,
first we must explode Europe to the clouds,
for until then are locked up and bolted shut
all those marvels and magic charms;
perhaps then, when the captain for a friendly handshake
will ferry the melancholy poet
to Africa, across the ocean, billowing with fierce waves
into tropical climates, thousands of miles away,
into a land of wondrous events and beauty,
    oh, Master John,
we will meet once more then, maybe, maybe,
on the shore of the Ivory Coast.

The Little Ring

There, at the curve in the road,
near the flowering jasmine,
a little silver ring I dropped,
I remember this often.

We recall this often, me and you,
a tiny stone fell from it,
it was like periwinkle, pale blue
on a stalk of green.

The two of us for it stooped low,
in the dust our hands met,
harebells in bloom would toll
and we both then wept.

They ring in the honeymoon
the harebells in bloom,
one another we chose,
and yet we parted soon.

Then a short time passed
and—this is how things go—
jasmine again blooms on the path,
and another now I hold.

There, at the curve in the road,
the memory is overgrown
a silver ring I no longer own,
instead I wear a ring of gold.

To my finger it has come to cling
so tightly, as you I may clasp,
Half my heart I may have lost,
yet I will not lose this little ring.

All the Beauties of the World

At night, the black skies of streets were ablaze with lights,
how beautiful were the ballet dancers on bills between black
    type,
low, very low gray aeroplanes like doves had swooped down
and the poet remained alone among flowers, stupefied.
Poet, perish with the stars, wither with the flower,
today no one will mourn your loss even for an hour,
your art, your fame will wane forever and decline,
because they resemble flowers in the graveyard;
for aeroplanes, which are fiercely soaring up to the stars,
in your stead now sing the song of steely sounds
and beautiful they are, just as lovelier are the jolly electric
    blossoms
on the houses in the street than the flower-bed variety.

For our poetry we found utterly new kinds of beauty,
you moon, island of vain dreams, burning out, cease to shine.
Be silent violins and ring you horns of automobiles,
may people crossing the street suddenly begin to dream;
aeroplanes, sing the song of evening like a nightingale,
ballet dancers, dance on bills between black typeface,
the sun may not shine,—from towers floodlights beam
into the street they will cast a new flaming day.

Falling stars were trapped in the iron constructions of lookout
    towers,
before the cinema screen today we dream our fairest dream,
the engineer builds bridges in the wide Russian plains
and high above the waters will travel our trains
and on rooftops of skyscrapers when the lights burn brightly,
we take walks, without feeling the need to recite poetry
and like a rosary during prayer between bony fingers will bead,
the elevator rises between floors a hundred times a day,

and gazing from above you will behold all the beauties of the
   world.
And that which was sacred art only yesterday
suddenly was transformed into things real and plain,
and the loveliest pictures of today were painted by no one,
the street is a flute and it plays its song from dawn till night
and high above the town to the stars aeroplanes glide.

Well then, adieu, allow us to leave you invented beauty,
the frigate heads for the distance across the open sea,
muses, let down your long hair in grief,
art is dead, the world exists without it.

For greater truth is even in this little butterfly,
which, from its cocoon, having gnawed the book of verse, will
   rise to the sun,
than in the poet's verses, which are written on each its page.

And that is a fact that no one can deny.

Afterword

Seifert is putting out a second book of poetry. And this epilogue we address to all those who liked *City in Tears*. For *Sheer Love* is almost cyclically connected with Seifert's debut, being its other hemisphere—and in technical terms both its expansion and its opposing pole. With these two books the first period of Seifert's development as a poet has been exhausted and completed.

Sheer Love has no traditions besides its own and the one that is the atmosphere of today's youth and today's revolution.

In terms of subject matter it is exclusively situated in the proletarian world. From it the collection draws a new creative spirit and a new boldness.

A new boldness!

This and the longing associated with it it sings. No one's fabricated illusions about the worker. It tears down the wretched martyrlike, pathetic nimbus with which he was endowed by the bourgeoisie and false socialist poets. It shows the worker in his true light.

It celebrates his most primitive physical dreams, which are: sacred ambrosia and sacred nectar in all secular forms. It celebrates his spiritual pleasures, which are: loyal love of the beloved and the child, enthusiasm about collectivity, respect for revolution, determination to sacrifice himself. It celebrates his social pleasures, which are: song, dance, play-acting, distant European and exotic homeland, all the beauty of the world, new beauty. It honors the fruit of his work from hammer to aeroplane. It celebrates his class hatred.

And the poet as a man and as an artist is entirely from the proletarian world.

His is absolute sincerity.

His instrument is the lyre and his broad, wavy rhythms have nothing in common with the rhetorical. Neither fleeing from reality nor into utopia, nor anywhere else, in his poetry there is romanticism of this great century. In his poems lives Kladno, lives New York—lives Paris, lives Jičín, Prague, the entire world.

His basic temperament is dreaminess. He has an admirable gift for linking literal, standard tendencies (political phrase, journalistic term) with an absolutely poetic and fantastic streak. His work has nothing to do with the current Philistine allegorical "tendentious" social poetry that today is produced wholesale with bourgeois intent of education, morality, and instruction.

And to conclude:

Sheer Love grew out of the revolutionary climate of Devětsil and is its authentic expression.

DEVĚTSIL

On the Waves of TSF

1925

To Teige, Nezval, and Honzl

Light grief on the face   Deep laughter in the heart

GUILLAUME APOLLINAIRE

We hate to remember things past   let us forget
yet looking up from the bottom of the street eyes upturned
I was thinking of You   poet
as you walked by years ago and said smiling: Shepherdess Eiffel
In autumn ships pass the city like languidly flowing years
where did Your Muse go when You said good-bye to Paris
I met a thousand women in the streets and none was so beautiful
but the star of Bethlehem Étoile still shines
I learn to write poems like a soldier learns to blow the bugle
when in the barracks window he puffs up his cheeks into golden metal
and drawn-out sounds flutter their wings flying across the streets
Paris is the mirror of Europe   in it I see Your smile
I rise   I rise   on this ladder to the stars
in iron boughs a pink ballet dancer plays the guitar
a tired butterfly reclines upon the roses in her hair
but too small is a day to encompass the whole city
from the Trocadéro window vaulted the moon   grinning murderer's face
and it is funny for all things in the world are beautiful
I embrace the stony breasts of the sphinx at the Louvre entrance
thinking of Your wife as she weeps over a book of verse
but the golden-yellow firecracker dies faster than it flared up
may not all poems be more beautiful any longer than this one
above the city of Your evenings that you loved so much
Your head in white bandages I see before my eyes forever
and it is funny   I am leaning on the mount of an old cannon
the darkness is closing before me the Guide to Paris
an Aeolian harp is Eiffel   hark the wind of events and beauty
it swells the sails of art   Oh dead helmsman

FIERY FRUIT

To love poets
the dying fauna of YELLOWSTONE PARK
and yet we love poetry
poetry
eternal waterfall

Long-range cannons were shelling Paris
poets in helmets
but why count the dead of unhappy love?
farewell Paris!

We were sailing around Africa
and fish with diamond eyes
were dying in the steamer's propellers
it hurts worst
when we reminisce
Black man's lyres
and the aroma of hot air
at home not before midnight ripens the fiery fruit of chandeliers
and Mr. Blaise Cendrars
lost a hand in the war

Sacred birds
like shadows on thin legs
sway the fate of worlds
Carthage is dead
and the wind plays sugarcanes
a thousand clarinets

And meanwhile on fragile parallels of the earth
           H I S T O R Y
           clings hundred-year-old ivy
I am dying of thirst Miss Muguet
           and you will not tell me
what wine might have tasted like in Carthage

The star was struck by lightning
           and it is raining
surfaces of waters
           tight drums whirled
revolution in Russia
           capture of the Bastille
and the poet Mayakovsky is dead

           but poetry
           a honied moon drips sweet juices
           into flower cups

Honeymoon

HONEYMOON

If it were not for those foolish kisses
we would not go on honeymoons
yet if it were not for the honeymoons
what good would Wagons lits do?

Unending anxiety of train station bells
wedding cars   ah Wagons lits
that marital bliss is like fragile glass
a honeyed moon is descending

My dear in the windows can you see the Alps
let's open the window for perfumes wide
see the sugar of snowdrops   supple snow of lilies
behind Wagons lits is Wagon restaurant

Ah Wagons restaurants   wedding cars
forever to be their guest and then to dream
about happiness in marriage over delicate cutlery
HANDLE WITH CARE! CAUTION GLASS!

And yet another night and yet another day
two beautiful days and two beautiful nights
Where is my train schedule that book of poetry
oh how beautiful are my railway cars

oh Wagons restaurants and Wagons lits

oh honeymoon

departure of a ship

I put on beautiful spectacles
which do not make me wise
Do you like almonds? Such moments
are the bitter almond of good-bye

Farewell you ship   beautiful ship
the waves are like hillsides steep
and pilots who guide you
like a shepherd a jingling sheep

I lost a tiny collar button
today I cannot leave
kindly tell my tender beauty
to stop coming to meet me

The girls wept   with them I wept
I also wanted to wave my handkerchief
they waved handkerchiefs bloodstained
with the red paint of rouge

And foreign countries beautiful lands
fine lace of beautiful danseuses
shepherds play their shawms
you can win more at a game of dice

Above the sea a policeman stands hesitant
perhaps he also wanted to say farewell
the rocky shore was bathing nude and bare
and he did not see her then.

Marseille

The fisherman leaning from the boat is fishing till dusk
fish are peculiar beauties red golden and alien
and octopi in the water so iridescent
completely vanish from your gaze in the mesh of the net
Woe to you stars silver coins unlocking the heavens
the pirate ship is already rising   moon in the sky
a little table sits next to you in the coffeehouse
like a flamingo standing on one leg asleep
by the sign of laughter those girls you will recognize
the surface of the sea is the mirror of stars and lights
black men at night are blacker still a hundred times
and you beauty before whom many have already knelt
your eyes are deep as the sea near the isle of If
I don't know if anyone could be found this night
who standing near you with you could resist sin
A year of one's youth the Count of Monte Christo
everyone has remembered certainly on the seashore
to be sure fish eyes are like your rocking horse's eyes
it was wooden and in them you could see your smile
like in the eyes of fish dead here in a pile
a hazy tiny star flickers in the clouds
33 jazzbands in the famous street Belsunce
with the new dawn one after the other grows silent
all harlots are now asleep   don't wake them from dreams
and next to each a black man   his dark hand
rests on their breasts with all its weight
as if a black spider enveloped their hearts
with an ominous web

harbor

ANCHOR   still one beautiful hope at the end
a dead oyster is ascending toward the ship

HELMSMAN   in the evening to walk about Marseille
on the shoes still the Singapore dirt

SHIP   in the rigging of the mast between lanterns
a parrot and a monkey thought they were at home

NIGHT   a soldier and a girl remained at the café alone
the bottle cast the shadow of Emperor Napoleon

SHIP'S PROPELLER   when to the dance everyone had gone
from the deep water lilies to the surface would float

CRANES   to sleep grotesque giraffes in long files moved on
along palm trees of a land unknown

sea

When from wanderlust we suffer
to ourselves we say:

SEA WAVES   *SEA WAVES*

in a rosy envelope our love we declare
and then kissing women's soft hair
to ourselves we say:

HAIR WAVES   *HAIR WAVES*

Girls were bathing in the sea early Sunday
the sea and their hair melt into one wave crest
the sailor begins to sing another melody
scanning the horizon in a crow's nest

Waves and waves ripple and ripple
and on shore they finally rest

MARBLE TOWN

The marble square of this town
like a flower bed of fluttering parasols
Lights flowers   flowers lights
and the sea a royal harp of glory
whispered with strings of waves sparkling
when sails like the cheeks of a girl singing
swell with wind filled with flowers

The town is sinking into mire slowly
in the spire hangs the sun a bell so golden
Love remained alone of glorious history
Flowers love and a Chinese lantern

Birds and sailors vie with each other in song
that light at sea it is not a blossom
it is not even a light it is a foreign liner
and like a fan of silver pearls the sky
conceals the moon's laughter

When a girl with the love star on her brow
sells you roses with a smile

And lovely she is when I picture her in my mind
Those breasts of hers so tiny it is almost funny
a dove could cover with one blue-gray wing

HÔTEL *"Côte d'Azur"*

And waves like backs of bitter fish
into the net of the sky
                when the fisherman dozes
on the seashore the hôtel *"Côte d'Azur"*

Memory of love   the sign of cancer
my sweet past
            and sweet pineapple
from the shell of evening Venus is born

And this goddess in a green tricot
on the wings of seagulls
             in a sailing boat
on waves of clouds across the night she rides

The painters' brushes already dried up with colors
oh poetry
        idle is the poet
while the girls are having their hair cut
my longings grow

And above the terrace the hôtel *Côte d'Azur"*
I am falling asleep
             into the net of dreams
red pineapple and yellow bananas
and waves like backs of bitter fish
          turned into art by magic

Sails
   and mint candy

Park

A stream of water like playful fingers
into stony lyre strings in the hands of POETRY
and the gardener
                        with his hose in the middle of the path
a poet has become

And became a grower of roses which he adores
he is dying of love while watering them
those roses
            Lady Waterloo and Star of France
in July *Snow Pearl*

When autumn comes
and the saddest blossoms of all
when lovers
                 around the basin
upside down will stroll

See Archimedes is drawing circles in the dirt
light rain is falling onto the fountain's spurt

MY ITALY

STO STAI STA STIAMO STATE STANO

In spite of broken wings angels fall headlong like meteors
onto roofs of hangars   the Renaissance skies are empty

FO FAI FA FACCIAMO FATE FANO

Along the Forum Romanum Mussolini on a motorcycle goes
Italian grammar's four irregular verbs see modern poetry

DO DAI DA DIAMO DATE DANO

Perhaps this is not a poem but whatever it may be
may it be say icy lemonade which is called Frappè

VO VAI VA ANDIAMO ANDATE VANO

or a confession of love in the garden Boboli.

Nightlights

O On which page in which dictionary
tender words of love would I find
for I am not a poet and the night closes in
on the silver crossroads and its light

L Sphinx moth night owl feelers of lights automobile
black carpet of night crescent among stars
The clock is singing night Before you if I kneeled
I would impress my likeness into your palms

L Open your hands and palms an angel spreading his wings
two chairs and on the table yellow lamplight
so that you are with me lay your lips on my cheek
a kiss long and lingering like a song Curtains of white

A

G Through the lace of tiny cushions we gaze into the street
Automobile sphinx moth of the silver crossroads night owl
and the child love's third star in the cradle falls asleep
You sing with your hand touching its white down

U Love is a prayer granted this very instant of grace
the world fades under the gaze like a movie scene
hold me close an angel with his own wings embraced
pleasure closes our eyes and we cannot perceive

M

S Like a distant storm screams of lights rage
the velvet shadow of your profile fell upon my hand
in which dictionary and on which page
would I find words of love worthy of a man

moon rose and raven

VERSES ABOUT TWO WHO DROWNED

That ship was like a crushed violin
and the sail like the torn-off wing of a bird
The last star was fading on the horizon
What happened? Sailors do you hear?
What happened sailors come on!

And it is too late Face of a woman so very young
it flows on the waves like a white water lily
lying flat on his back his hands spread out
a sailor follows her through the sea quietly

Dolphins scare shy mermaids
above the salty wave a seagull chokes with laughter
dead one whereto are you drifting on the waves
like a white water lily with a dead sailor

Cutlery already chimes at the resort restaurant
like birds awakened under the palm tree
Ah a horn is the upturned trunk of an elephant
which is melting a tone like gold in its deep

An Englishman yawns in a sail of Daily-Mail
a silver wave is turning an empty shell
a bunch of grapes lies on a crystal plate
and from a melon drops of blood well

But suddenly like an empty glass the flute fell from lips
horrified the bird cried and a wave swept the shell away
a lady fainted upon white table linen
and then talk in the restaurant stopped

And the dead floated to the feet of the Englishman
his monocle to the ground he dropped

Frozen Pineapples

and other lyrical anecdotes

Evening at the café

Princess Salome you are strolling through my
dream
I see your head of hair between goblets and
grapes
oh what bliss a poet to be
to be a poet with the eyes of an eccentric

The waiter carries his head on a silver tray

I want to hide from the world like a mouse in
the sand
where did that banner on the red ship's mast
cruise
and why is the anchor a sign of hope if here I
feel so sad
and that song will not awaken the dead
danseuse?

Under an artificial palm a smiling black man
on his face a rose-colored mask of light
At that moment the great love in my heart I
overcame
yet her shadow follows me through the night

Through the night   across a hanging garden
                              of withered stars
when I adventurer of beauty and passionate
                              sleeper
leaning on the heat of an American stove as
                              if to sleep forever
                              I desired
remembered frozen   pineapples

Crests of chrysanthemums like light ostrich
                              feathers
on the table cards   fate   loves   burden

ECCENTRIC

Snow forever white   and forever you must love her
when white flowers of fog were falling onto the quay
resembling pierrot   half light half dark my features
                                       I feel sleepy

love iron rings in granite on the quay

Are you thinking of Marseille? Tambourines
A white dove brings a letter with a double seal
there is many a pretty thing that we love to see
when in the pocket the last crown will ring!

Smoke from a small steamer's stack that you fancy
is it you making breakfast for yourself Captain Sir?
and we thought of whales of argosies and of the sea
in the wind of waves shiver trembling coral reefs

Why are you so very sad adventurous lady?
Your sadness of glass entrust into a man's hands
already a pale star entered the window   roosters sang dawn
                                                                early
You are my witness in wine cups withered petals of rose

cold tears under a threefold laughter's mask
oh eccentric!

resembling pierrot who is feeling sleepy
I know for love men with rapiers will fight
after all you must love her forever forever
snow forever white

ALL PERFUMES

At the magnificent springs of "Eau de Cologne"
flowers were shaking off their powder airy pollen
This was the spa of ailing beauties alone
bathing in the silver of mirrors

And in the colonnades fauna of musical instruments
to the rhythm of the song uncoils a snake
That melody I know
to that melody all Europeans should dance and sway

To dance around the small piano
long to sniff at blossoms on the girl's hat
and then taste taste the honey of flaxen hair
when on white pillows it will flow

mirror square

Mirror square of frozen sea portrait in the deep
without fragrance an underwater flower blossoming
in the mirror a smile   it is not you or is it
maybe she is still asleep fair beauty Omaki Vani

Sparkling lemonade of stars flows to earth from the skies
and the word like a golden coin will echo
Behind the blue screen may I only behold the tender shadow
and for three words of love I will buy smiles

An electrifying comb in a palm so tiny
the hand is rising   the hand is sinking
to live without love fair Omaki Vani
Telegraphy without wires   Airplanes without an engine

Bleeding wings before me
Horror shaking the earth and Yokohama in ruins
Omaki Vani fair beauty
I am afraid for your tall hairdo with the long pins

Miss Gada-Nigi

Night   extended raven wings   drum of darkness
Miss Gada-Nigi perched on the trapeze
below in the sand the clown like a bird asleep
                    the snow of his dreams falling

Gada-Nigi smiles at the stars through a crack in the canvas
listening to the ticking of the watch on her wrist
she learns to dance on the head of a rearing steed
and in the lace of fog eternity between stars

Ticking watch   on the clown's face reflection of infinity
in the circus wagon a child broke into tears
hands reaching out for the stars of mother's breasts
and bird song was swaying on the branch of jasmine

when backs turned the lovers and the suicidal man
under the luminous parasol of the streetlamp
they saw a star falling through a thousand-year-old night
as it died among the water lilies of the shallow basin

Oh Miss Gada-Nigi do not contemplate the stars
for the lines of the hand enclose fate the clown me and you
only lovers die of love unwittingly   just listen
in a kiss two slim flutes of breath fell silent

CIRCUS

Today for the first time John the famous fire-eater
pressed the little dancer Chloe to his chest

AND LITTLE CHLOE WAS STILL A VIRGIN

Pom the clown that same night outside the circus
sent out to the audience to greet them a

BIG BALLOON

TODAY FOR
THE LAST TIME

King Herod

WHEN HE RAISED A GRAPE TO HIS LIPS
HEROD KING MURDERER OF INNOCENTS
ON HIS HAND TERRIBLE TRACES OF
                              BLOOD

BUT WHAT KIND OF SIN BURDENS YOUR
                              SOUL
ON YOUR HAND TERRIBLE TRACES OF
                              BLOOD
WHEN YOU RAISED A GRAPE TO YOUR
                              LIPS

ICE CREAM POETRY

Pass me that bouquet of snow roses
It is already spring at the North Pole?
Oh no it's only angels with wings of snow
and one may think   Why not?

This isn't snow that flake of handkerchief
I already see the window in the pipe's white mist
laugh you people standing under eaves
laugh my gentle manikins

On the roofs of houses sweet ice cream
all that you see here is beautiful so
eyes of glass are melting with tears
these are no tears of laughter   Oh no

It is already spring at the North Pole
and one may think   Why not?

Wisdom

all those loves that caused hearts to bleed
were only silly foolishness

in the end we will love our long pipe

black swan

Lightbulb

Around the cold light of bulbs
whirling wings' tireless buzz

And Mr. EDISON
having raised his eyes from a book he was reading
        smiles
He has saved the lives of a vast number of moths!

beauty

You say that the manikin is smiling ironically
in the crystals of the hairdresser's window?
Forever beautiful she watches the wrinkles of aging beauties
who visit her twice a week

Rebus

RASCAL LUCK

RASCAL LUCK

RASCAL LUCK

RASCAL LUCK

RASCAL LUCK

(The greater the rascal—the greater the luck)

DISCOVERIES

In the year 1492 the Genoese Christopher Columbus discovered unknown islands

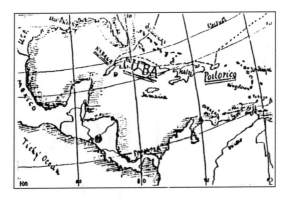

Thank you Sir!

I smoke cigarettes!

Street

Squint your eyes when walking the street at night
[from your office]
each lamp for hair has long beams of light
which you would in vain try to see then

with your eyes open

Eyes

OOh daisy eyes OOh daisy eyes
   how lovely they are!
it's only poor students who must
   wear specs to graduate

Fan

A GIRL'S BLUSH TO CONCEAL
COQUETTISH EYES   A DEEP SIGH
IN THE END WRINKLES AND A BITTER SMILE

ON THE BREASTS A BUTTERFLY
PALETTE OF LOVE
WITH COLORS OF FADING MEMORY

ABACUS

○ Your breast

is like an apple from Australia

● Your breasts

are like 2 apples from Australia—

how I like this abacus of love!—

Poet

he sang and sang of sadness
of youth which is dead
while on his chin there were still traces
of the milky way

NEW YORK

THIS IS NOT THE MAIDEN OF
  ORLEANS
THIS IS THE FAMOUS STATUE OF
  LIBERTY
WHICH BEARS THE TORCH AND
  SCORCHES
THE AIRPLANE'S WINGS

NAPOLEON

MY GAMBIER PIPE ENTERTAINS
  ME GREATLY
THE EMPEROR'S HEAD IS ITS
  FUNNY BOWL

GOOD DAY FAMOUS EMPEROR!

  HAS THE DREAM OF RULING
    THE WORLD
  AT LAST EVAPORATED FROM
    YOUR HEAD?

miss miss your face is gloomy
because it rained on you all day
but what should that little

May fly say
whose whole life was filled with rain?

Love

those dying of cholera
exhale the aroma of
   May lilies
inhaling the aroma of
   May lilies
we are dying of love

remember the wise philosophers

life is nothing but a moment

and yet when we were awaiting our beloved

it was eternity

Words on magnet

Up until the equator a white bear sleeps on floating ice
in the polar circle a bird from the tropics dies
the night cracked open like a nut at midnight sharp
white star

In the exotic aquarium the water has frozen to the bottom
golden fish do not move between fragile limbs
and in mid-January paper roses have blossomed
The glassy hemisphere of night is falling

House amidst a park   purple crystal from afar
even may the boughs of trees be as bare and plain
as perches for stuffed birds in the school cabinet
or a beggar's cane

Spring is returning love letter from Menton
in the shirt pocket melted the frozen seal
the magical nuances of perfumes do you know
in one limpid drop the aroma of spring

Carnival masks vanish into the dark street startling rats
a shower of confetti falls on slim windowsills into the snow
and words   remnants of stars tumbling into silence
from the broken record on the gramophone

The fragile glass of winter is full of violet flair
like my girl's hair into lyrical hairdos I want to braid verses
indeed have you not found in the park on a forlorn trail
girls' lost hairpins?

How can I tell the maidens about the world war and fright
Let history paint the scene Battlefield palette is bloodstained
Play of words   Antennas grazing the sky
and the last word of my poem is number *two hundred forty-eight*

! ! HELLO ! !

Since fauns elves and dryads suffered extinction
it was necessary to invent the telephone! Hello!
that love of yours is driving me to desperation
    a swallow is sitting on the telephone pole

At dusk when the dew has cooled wither will the flower
but from the famous Capitol to Manhattan's skyscrapers
the beauty of women has not withered even for an hour
    in the snow of exotic powders and vapors

To be sure the lovesick are sustained by poetry
and for you the gramophone your love will bemoan
after all candymaker Love from vanilla he makes ice cream
    and is shivering with the cold

The cuckoo in the clock a hundred times has called
On the icicle flute an aria I blow
See starry notes that song is already old
    in Paris there is the magasin Printemps

And in the Radio bar a drunken pilot wagers
that he will reach the stars before you finish your cigarette
What countless pleasures life could allot
    but poets do not have wings

And if it were not for grief love's sickness afflicting me
I would mix my pleasures like cards and cocktails
how sad would the funeral be for the brothers Fratellini

pierrot with a lute and boston

The thief and the clock

Forever running are the clock and the thief
poetry is the art of losing precious time
Better to seek eternal verities
and heed my warning words of advice

HAVEN'T YOU FORGOTTEN TO WIND UP YOUR WATCH?

The cock sometimes crows and sometimes it fires a gun
those who tried to lead were led astray
And as Moses once led the Jews through the desert
we have electrical leads

IS YOUR PIANO WELL-TUNED?

because being well-attuned is a gift from God
who feeds us daily with honeycombs
Too bad that no one resembles him
so that we might not feel sad in the street of Mirth

with a coquettish lady

With a coquettish lady himself in jockey attire
on horseback in the park For a first rose he reaches
the lady is a muse when she offers a smile
and backwards she kisses his lips

And in his office like a fencer
the rival with a fencing mask in the mirror
rapier in hand the hurled rose he pierces
in a hazardous wager

This is my heart   wails the lady
adieu my beautiful dream
The poet is lost in reverie and in a while
through his mirror image he runs a rapier

Concert café

Maneuvering dreadnought
meets a violin on the waves
the captain's hat flew away
circling the ship   White bird

However the violin bow
powered by warm currents
was borne to unknown islands
into the rotting water of coves

Under our skies
only paper palms survive
shells of empty streets
on the bottom of evenings

There among balmy scents
the black king of the island
is enthroned bow in his hands

There the heads of his subjects
dance around him in a circle wide
like the black dots of crotchets

and from the grasses snakes spring
in the curve of the treble clef

Violin only softly you may sing
Europe is sleepy   is sleepy
and stars she will fling

LAWN-TENNIS

Forget your dark thoughts
and heavy hearts
Remember white lawn-tennis
and light rubber balls

Oh old guitars and mandolins
histories are dead and wandering knights
Listen to the racquets' wailing strings
in wicker easychairs

CIGARETTE SMOKE

bite of the viper
venomous pallor   moon
poetry
malady of black men and monkeys

and this malady
soft pillow of ennui
icy compresses for the night
when vicious fevers alight

cigarette smoke
rises
tourist in the Alps
the sun and the deep

above a steep ravine
the Montblanc peak
acrobatics of roses
from clouds

it rises to the stars
which are drunk by
the pillow of ennui

poetry

Fever

Eyes half-closed
sinking into the softness of dreams and down
the patient dozed:

snow   spider   rose

The nurse comes in the twilight
closes the window of the summer night
and the moon yellow crab creeps along the pane

blood mercury and perfume

On coconut matting shadows are playing
take Africa's temperature
in hell of ague devils are dying

glaciers have a fever

When the patient raises his eyes from the deep of dreams
an unknown girl at his bedside arrives
and carries a white flower between her teeth

how might it smell?

Oh no It is only a phantom and it is laughable
the label of the medicine on his table:
death carries a white dagger between the teeth

Fate

We used to play chess on terraces of cafés
black white checkers Like the chessboard of night
squares of pillows and of darkness black and white

We could not help but think of Longchamp
the rearing horses however did not run farther
than to Your fingers which I adore

Your nails the color of early spring flowers
the distance from lips to lips Kiss
                              Tomorrow morning

Yet what good were my castles and pawns
It happened in midsummer on terraces of cafés
and it was the game of love

Rue de la Paix

When diamond dew gleams
on frail ivory
in glass tamed wild beasts

a bird of paradise fleeing from them
alighted on a bed of incense
Leopards wolves and polar bears

When the glacier of silky fabrics
with inwoven flora floats away
and pearls explode in its wake

here beggars' faces are glued to glass
as if life were a desert
before this oasis of beauty in hostile lands

And weeping for the lot of misery
into five pieces the girl broke
the hard crust with a bit of dry loaf

Are rains the perfume of the sky
then tears are the perfume of the soul
on Friday and Sunday I saw her cry

With her tears I will scent my handkerchief
this very day

Graveyard in Genoa

A ship rolls in
and on shore
a sailor sprawls
and remains prone

How far to the graveyard?

Six tapers
a team of swans
takes you
to the tomb

Lifefarers   seafarers

Two ports
oh Genoese
The sea is swelling
and will not cease

Life and sea   Life and sea

Silken handkerchief

TO SEE HANDS TYING SNOWDROPS
SNOWDROP BUD HALFBLOOM FLOWER
VISITING CARD OF SPRING
MONOGRAM OF POETRY WHITE STRING

WHY DO GIRLS SMILE IN WINDOWPANES
WHICH ARE WEEPING IN THE APRIL RAINS
THE TREE BOOMS LIKE A HARP SWAYING
WITH SWEET MUSIC

PALE HANDS IN A GIRL'S LAP
WITH A FLOWER AS IF BREATHED ONTO GLASS
MAY I NEVER SEE AGAIN THE PLASTER CAST
ON THE PIANO OF BEETHOVEN'S HANDS

A WORLD FULL OF HORROR FULL OF BEAUTY TENDER
AT LAST LET ME FORGET AND REMAIN FOREVER ALONE
A RING WITH A PEARL IN A SEAWEED TANGLE
VISITING CARD MONOGRAM

PATENT LEATHER PUMPS AND HEAVY ARTILLERY

To be a fisherman

To be a fisherman in the Sahara
and a bottomless ship's captain
look that is all that will remain
but it is not important here

We say: photos of dead sweethearts
this is sadder than Pompeii
a tiny bunch of dry lilies of the valley
            when it is May

We say: everything is dead
this is sadder than Pompeii
photographs of dead sweethearts
            when it is May

And that's all that will remain

This muttering stanza
is my final rhyme
Each year we have our usual influenza
and for days we cry

The Nightingale Sings Poorly

1926

The nightingale sings poorly—Jean Cocteau

To the painter Josef Šíma

Moon on Wings

Hyacinth flower
the pope's crown
the pope sleeps now
his beauty sleep

Behold my pipe
cloud of incense
hyacinth bud
suits me well

Night full of beauty
moon turned pale
the airplane
broke its wing

Death hangar of peace
Thrust from the sky
Thermometer mercury
gushed to the ground

Angel of mourning
over this wreck
of pinions of wings
weeps with yearning

You love of mine
sweet surf tide
The moon plays
the guitar shines

The Hourglass

The pyramid is glowing
oasis of shadows crystal of history
A venomous fly is guarding
the corpse of the queen

Famous sleepers!
them will not disturb
the vulture that circles
the sphinx is mute

A centennial spider weaves
a web of some density
Behold what ennui rages
in the Egyptian city

French-made cars
pass us by
the beautiful name
captivates no one

Citroën?
Pineapple and stars
and here sweet wine
Where are you Egyptian woman?

Placid to remain
like the midnight moon
Europe never again
will my eyes behold you

Departing automobiles
cannot go farther than the shore
At the end of the universe
a will-o'-the-wisp dies in a shrub

Those not afraid to ride
saddle the sphinx they may try
the surf tide of time
breaks against her breasts

The highest score contestants
is death!

Verses

With whom to be lonely, with whom to be alone
and gape over the abyss?
And weep? Old Abraham once shed tears
and an angel ascended in an ermine cloak.

I don't know where the north is, the compass lies
and all girls equivocate,
Go to the fork in the road, the pole will indicate
three paths at once.

A strong smell wafts from hairdos of Jewesses,
those are comets sweeping.
My eyes are circling in nothing but ellipses,
which cannot be seen.

We have forgotten the muses,
they do not have wings.
To have medusas, oh medusas, for lovers,
whose kisses are embers.

From corals a staff and then go one's way,
where sepias rule,
to taste the milk of the whale,
that someone may pour.

Adieu, adieu, adieu!

A Song about Death

Die we must
even if unwillingly
The voice of the knell
is dying Unwillingly

Pearls and jewels
to the living we return
like the suicide from the bottom
bubbles of air

And so we die needy
we die ordinary
with gold teeth
in a white gum

Perhaps it is only a smile
of pure gold
It is not as fearsome
as we are told

What does death mean
May it whet its scythe
When the thrush sighs
it is sleeping

Spiral
oh elastic spring
Why are you weeping
my aspiring one

when the thrush sighs
and sleeps?

Ancient Wisdom

A dog-rose climbing vine
has caught a butterfly
A dog has begun to howl
softly tinkled a small glass of wine

The girl resembles the butterfly
Too bad all the pollen dust
When the Archipelago bursts into flames
the fire is mirrored by the waves

Jules Verne died
Never mind The astonishing adventure is alive
Buried treasures
the moon and fear of reptiles

Don't be afraid We have peace
and sweet good cheer
The rose petal in the sink
races against the hand on the clock

So calmly to learn to live
in deep-seated and bitter wisdom
motionless crab
in deep-sea blueness of the ocean

Rose petal rose petal
rosy sheet the ship and her sail
May shy girls blush with shame
and weep

14th of July

Asleep is the venerable Mr. Mirabeau
so is the history of barricades
in Jardin des Plantes sleeps the marabou
the most melancholy of birds

On July fourteenth
revolution and the street
Mr. Mirabeau in his wig
Marie is playing the violin

Who is this Marie?
The marabou
drinks muddy water
wiser than Mr. Mirabeau

Indeed from barricades wine flows
and naughty Marie
likes bars Whoever likes colors
loves the cap of liberty

When the poet invented the calembour
oh calembour
the boulevard exploded with laughter
His feathers ruffles the marabou

Oh Marie! To the Jardin des Plantes
soared a solitary marabou
and God knows where Mirabeau went
reciting that calembour

Girlfriends

This year for the last time
we celebrate Christmas.
Gisèle and Emma
are holding hands.

A round table
and a bouquet for the ladies
A shade of sorrow on cheeks,
sundial.

Little Gisèle
suddenly weeps.
Those aren't bells,
those are my loafers.

I am sitting by the stove
quietly writing verse:
at the North Pole, Mr. Amundsen,
is sitting there in a fur coat.

Fire burns in the stove.
But how much so!
On the ceiling roams
a red flamingo.

It has a nest in the fiery heat.
Emma has a dream:
strangle it, strangle it,
pluck out its feathers!

Gisèle turns pale,
horror of horrors,
those aren't shades,
those are spiders.

Revolver in hand,
aim at the corner!
Shoot at the spider's heart,
kill the spider!

No, I will not kill it,
it I know.
Glistening in its silken threads I saw
a false diamond.

On the bosom a rose
for three sous.
From its web the spider will weave us
a mask for the ball.

Paravent

The singer has stepped on the mandolin
fig full of juice
The Chinese straightens his eyes and kisses a European woman
in the folds of his robe a dragon crunches chocolate

The European woman
with two rosy fingers she slants each eye
smiling at the Chinese man
in the mirror of snowy night

Seashell Vase of porcelain
with wet lilies
From blossom to blossom from ship to ship on the sea
lemon eyes

From star to star a tightened string
azure zither of the sea
The woman caresses her own breasts and cannot sleep
behind the paravent.

Yellow, Blue, Red

We are seeking a girl without prejudice, without a mask
in the café between glasses and stalks of straw in them soaking.
They are like cornflowers between wheat
and we pass them on the unplowed ridge.

It is a certain art,
I'd say, it is tightrope walking,
for above us is an abyss with floating icebergs,
sprinkled with bitter stars.

Then comes autumn,
it is hardly ever anything new or peculiar,
a cold, lime-blossom tea and sitting at the fire,
yet we always marvel at all this again.

Yellow, blue, red leaves in the parks,
ladies in their colorful robes readily resemble chameleons,
it is, then, actually mimicry,
so they are not seen by their husbands, when them they deceive.

Ah, the little, dear black page boy,
he knows all there is to know and so he smiles,
standing silently at his lift like a thermometer
with black mercury.

The lift is falling, the lift is climbing between floors,
a melancholy rosary
and we are ascending in it, escaping our sweethearts,
who pursue us with their kisses,

as far as the rooftops,
where from starched air artificial roses bloom,
that no one sees.

Panorama

The stag is retreating, the smoke of his antlers rising,
behind the leaf of fern listen to the star
and softly, only softly.

Plates replete with fruit and nights of stars,
I would like to pass you this bronze plate
and become a barber.

Oh hairdressers,
weary hands are gliding on smooth hair,
the comb is falling, the sculptor dropped his chisel
and in the mirror eyes have frozen.

Night has fallen. You are asleep?
Shatter the softness of your featherbeds!
Midnight hour. Electric lamps.
Dark, light, dark half-light
and see:

the mountain crest combs the sky's shock of hair
and stars are falling like golden lice.

Giant Mountains

A photographic camera on a delicate tripod,
a chamois with a single big eye.
I am no rifleman, I am scared,
a hundred times wounded by love.

From the well of a girl's hair her lover drinks,
well, these are only foolish things, only love.
The river accompanies us silently,
the guitar the song.

A fir tree halved by lightning, blown-out window of cathedrals.

Don't be alarmed my girlfriends,
like a battery of cannons amid profound peace
the earth slumbers below the mountains.

If I only knew which words will befall me,
when the snow falls!
The lumberjack alone can hew silence with his ax
and from the deep of the wood fairy tales will rise.

Adieu, Krakonoš, it is so sad,
Your boots we are fleeing across enchanted land.
And our buses smell of Paris
like snowdrops of spring.

Bread and Roses

The world stretched out between two poles
like muleskin
Between two things life
                    bread and roses

The world drones Drums drone
For puny things a great war
Victor and vanquished home they go
How far how far
is home

A pair of dice two magic words
in the cornet of history bread and roses
On the overturned drum play again
fiercely shaking the cornet in your hand

On the muleskin of the war drum
for our love hunger and dying

Ballad

The mill is grinding penury,
eyes in tears cling.
On the dead point
a dead man is sleeping.

The drum reverberates
and tears take its place on the way.
On four mill blades
penury scrapes.

Of white gauze
is the bride's wedding dress
and she weeps,
that with a deceased she will sleep.

War is coming, war is coming,
endlessly time is turning,
winters come, springs come,
Decembers and Mays.

The plow of war is plowing deep
the flowery land
and the surface of the sea,
which to blood is turning.

What will grow from the furrow,
when bloody seeds you have sown?
The sky has thundered and killings rise,
yet no end in sight.

An exploded grenade,
I will take the empty fragment
and will come you to congratulate
on your wedding banquet.

I will raise it aloft,
like a glass in a toast,
blood will flow
onto our heads.

Under the dark star
the land of people is consumed.
The mill reaches woefully into the sky
like a throne of penury.

Old Battlefield

The sun is turning the shade of things,
wind blades are breaking delicate mills.
We are in the land of fools, come, let's dance
once, twice.

How come in the graveyard we may dance
between life, between death?
Why not, why not, my danseuse,
in the land of fools?

The little foot soldier in trenches of fragrant soil
his rifle makes a cross over his head.
For the last time he falls asleep in his helmet,
good-night!

The king falls from his throne and the throne collapses,
false prophets are raising their voices,
that in the mouth of cannons birds are building nests
and the birds have left.

Under the tower battlement a horse's shadow races
for its emperor, for his shadow.
Dead are friends, dead are foes,
dead we are all.

Is it the land of fools and who is its master?
The carnival has begun, esteemed masks!
In gas masks we will not perish
in clouds of gas!

The sun is turning the shade of things,
the earth is pregnant with the dead.
Already it is bursting, come and let's dance
right around!

It is night, it is morn, and in the fog it is dawning,
shrouded in rags they all sleep.
It is the cloak of harlequin, the land, collapsed chessboard,
it is EUROPE.

A Ballad from the Champagne

4,000 French poets fell
in the world war.
"Temps"

On the palate you taste wine
and in wine I delight,
tell me Josephine,
how do you like the Champagne?

Your father was a vintner,
it was in the war.
It is long ago, you recall,
how he walked the vineyard in a hat of straw.

A bottle sits on the table
its neck delicate,
as I drink, of blood I must think,
of something frightfully sad.

Early one day
in her embrace her dad passed away,
she wept little Josephine,
but time is the sweetest remedy.

It was a horrible day,
worse followed, war came, soldiers came.
Cannons they dug in between grapes in the vineyard.
Josephine, are you still sad?

Josephine walked out to the vineyard,
she was alone.
A soldier saw her there: what's your name girl?
His arm around her waist, he jingled his spur.

*

Josephine's brother is growing up fast,
the war has long, long since passed,
It is plain—like his father he walks
the vineyard in a hat of straw.

Softly singing, he studies the grapevine,
fragile stalks he ties up with bast.
How heavy full bunches of grapes are,
when they ripen.

Evening comes, a star sweetens the sky,
the young vintner is homeward bound,
on his way one star has given him light,
and when he arrives, there are a thousand.

He is eating supper silently drinking wine,
in the paper he is looking quietly reading.
Have you seen yet, dear Josephine,
how many poets fell in France?

Four thousand!
The things that war will perpetrate!
Josephine is silent. In the silence,
now and then between teeth a glass of wine will resound.

She reminisces. Half smiles, half tears
make her lips tremble lightly.
—How many others there must have been
who did not know how to write poetry!

The Parting Kiss

Beautiful ladies were kissing
American volunteers.

I will never forget
that which I witnessed on that day,
the windows of cathedrals rattled,
at Verdun high were the flames.

The war was burning like a beacon,
trees shook down to their roots.
Above me it is not the firmament,
it's the door to the world's sanitarium.

Like empty tin cans of preserve
people rust here and putrefy.
From a loophole I gaze at the stars,
I am fighting for France.

For France?
A land I have never before seen!
So why do I take up my carbine,
why am I aiming to shoot and kill.

It rains on the dead,
delirious eyes in veils of yellow gauze,
I gaze in their eyes,
the dead face as if he cries.

It rains on the living,
delirious eyes in the helmet's shade,
why do I gape, why am I here,
when I feel so sad?

For sweet France?
Could she taste better than my home?
I don't know her women,
I have never tried her wine.

For the kiss of one little miss,
at home across the sea, at home;
when I went to war,
she touched my face with her lips.

She put her hand in mine, I pressed it
and lost was I,
I was so needy, I was starved,
her ring I kissed.

Shall I blame her,
to embitter my memory, tasting so sweet
shall I curse her, shall I weep,
or laugh heartily?

World war, break loose,
Rumble cannons buried in the soil!
For the kiss of one little miss,
I will be silent, I will be mute.

An Apple Tree with Cobweb Strings

Ruddy apples
have bent the regal stem like a harp,
autumn has draped it with cobweb strings,
wail and play
        my player!

We are not from that land where oranges ripen,
where grapevine twines around Ionic columns,
its grapes sweeter
        than the mouths of Roman women;
we only have the apple tree, warped severely
        by fruit and age.

And beneath this apple tree would sit he,
        who perhaps had seen
Parisian nights, Italian afternoons
        or the moon above the Kremlin,
home he returned all this to remember.

        In verse
a soft and serene melody, which could be played
in those spider's strings,
        I overheard.

Where to go for beauty,
        the sea, cities, and mountains,
where will trains take you for your peace
        to heal wounds that are still smarting?
        Where?

The gazes of women
and their breasts which would swing
your head into a lush and exotic dream,
           are not enticing?
A voice, redolent of far horizons, beckons,
           your land is small!

       Do you want to remain silent,
when temptingly it speaks to your yearning?

       It is after noon,
one fruit I will pick from the apple tree
           and long smell at it.

       To be alone,
beyond women's tears and beyond their smiles,
           to be home, solitary,
when a familiar song resounds in the boughs.

For the idle beauty of foolish women
           an apple is wasted.

Three Bitter Seeds

To Konstantin Biebl

Three bitter seeds
as a keepsake I received,
I wave a handkerchief
as a sign of grief.

As a farewell gift
three orange seeds,
into white handkerchiefs
people weep.

I planted them in a pot
watering them diligently,
for it's poetry, Italy's export,
to the cold homeland.

Good! They have grown.
How they bloom I don't know,
crimson, blue, yellow
ashen blossom?

the flaming blossom
will fade soon.
On the stalk green fruit clings
like bitter tears.

Who is weeping, whose tears are they?
From the seeds you gave me,
my orange
grew but did not ripen.

Well here it is not at home
that precious blossom,
all here must seem foreign
like frost.

The sun is chilly
the soil is different,
dew will fall
and a strange winter come

and a foreign spring.

       ●

A letter flew in from afar.
Where in the world is Java?
I reminisce about your little seeds
and here the snow is falling.

Why write about it, if one does not know?
On the ocean float glowing isles.
Hop, gentle words leap like monkeys
on the page into quatrains.

And in vain to my ear I lift my cane of bamboo,
it is silent, mute
and where would I drink milk of coconut,
if our cow does not have it.

    À propos,
    do in their ears black women there
    flowers and parakeet feathers wear?

So how do you fare in the rosy place?
I believe it is the eternal craving
of my little trees in the window glass,
which shiver,

when they feel the snow falling outside;
just so, transplanted into different soil,
you are one of the seeds of mine
in wistful separation.

For it must feel strange to you that hot cradle of earth,
in which blossoms sway
while birds are singing in the middle of our winter
when frost glazes our sun.

It is in vain that I water my trees
and vain to breathe warmth on faded leaves.
To sink into sleep, sleep like a snake may sleep
and suddenly at home to awaken,

when it is spring!

Moscow

It is long since they danced the minuet
and long since the harp has last played.
The glass cases in the old palace
have become tombstones for the dead.

There were battlefields,
the bloodied Kremlin wall still bares its teeth.
Bear us witness, you who are dead,
buried in velvet.

Glasses emptied of wine,
banners lowered over these past times,
a sword that tries to recall
from whose fist it did fall.

Rotten rings, a moldy diadem,
A collier, which still smells sweetly.
Decayed robes of dead czarinas
with an eyeless mask, a stare of death and damnation.

On the floor lies the czar's orb, emblem of authority,
rotten and worm-eaten.
This is the end, it is over under golden domes,
death guards the burial grounds of history.

Suits of armor, empty like golden nuts,
on carpets of singular designs
and Empire coaches travel backward into the past,
no horses, no passengers, no lights.

A Song about Moscow

The false little teeth of your domes
in snowy gums they shine.
Factories puff and smoke
in a circle wide.

We don't care a straw for diamonds
and for your glittering gold.
Nowadays we pay with bread
ready in hand.

Skilled jewelers,
leaning on their kneading troughs,
work liquid gold
and make round loaves.

How delicious it smells
this gem so poor and plain,
when the sliced half
a mother takes to her children.

And in their metal voice bells
announce to the entire land
in a deep bass:
Bread! Bread!

Gold is worthless!

At Our Lady of Iberia

From things religious to secular,
from prayer even to crime.
At Our Lady of Iberia
on the walkway there is a bazaar.

A Lenin badge for a ruble.
Give me one, little blue-eyed girl;
others have it and none of them is poorer,
I will buy the badge too!

Paintings, lamps, a horseshoe, a pot,
all the things waiting here for us.
The place looks as if a cannon shot
had demolished a bourgeois palace.

The phonograph is staunchly silent
it cannot sing revolutionary songs,
likely it remembers the moment
when it played for a noble miss.

Against the wall someone leaned a rapier,
it may be broken, but not deceased,
gone is its spring, which it had
once in the hand of a cavalier.

Old books piled on a heap,
oh what wisdom each of them may keep.
Dostoevsky's despair they hold,
there Pushkin's passion is growing cold.

It is turning inside out here
a past that will never reappear;
here workers tread, here soldiers tread
and women in bandannas of red.

Then there is something amusing,
so delightful and white as snow,
for the ladies brassieres of silk
are strung up on a long pole.

The Kremlin wall is gloomy and bloody
back there it is mute and grudging,
right beside it they are offering
that trifle that is all finery.

But I know, now I know
Jeanne d'Arc I remembered,
as she marches to battle in silver armor
and a sword and beauty crown her head.

They too are armor those brassieres
for maiden's hearts and breasts.
Love's armor, before it is pierced
by a lover's hands.

Lenin's City

The former palace of the admiralty,
An Empire conch, of which Venus was born
with a sailor's cap.
It was a small miracle.

That's all.

The harbor commander welcomes a Chinese captain
they are shaking hands. The white the yellow.
The ships stuffed with butter, chocolate, and tea
lie at anchor unmoving.

It is night. Like a drunken spider with a cross on its back
the monster cathedral staggers in the darkness.
In the colonnade, among black icons
the clamor of revolutions thunders.

The Winter Palace is colored with blood.
The marble column magnetizes the moon.
Blood flowed here. Snow is falling. Red and white.
At night it horrifies.

City on the Neva. Metropolis of poets.
The saber wrote red verses on your walls.
Instead of love words here cannons roared.
It was the revolution.

That's all.

Lenin

To the end of glory

The ruins of palaces have crumbled
    on cracked columns which will molder away
    to the end of glory.

That was Russia which we beheld,
    when the Kremlin's golden domes burned
    like candles on a coffin.

And meanwhile Moscow
    rippled on the wings of banners
    her streets boomed with the labor of worker's hands,
    until walls began to burst.

Full of grapes, full of life
    it was a charming village
    atop the ruins of Pompeii

While below peace reigned
    and death,
    under the paws of cats marble dust
    of antique sculptures.

•

In a chaise longue
already seriously ill and old
like a frail shadow and an old tree
Lenin reposed.

Death is drawing near
and little time remains,
a few sunny autumn days
and winter.

His face turned to where glow
the mirrors of Montblanc,
he beheld the world's face, he sees Europe
and the struggle of classes.

A bird, shot down,
plunges amazed into the willow brush
and in underground vaults of banks, where grows
that gold bullion in coils,

dogs, lazily trailing along the columns,
guard well the golden marshes,
over white sheets of paper, between ciphers
blood is gushing.

He sees cities and masses in motion
spilling over like a black shadow
in the glow of lights
and he hears the song, that he loved so dearly.

It is not a love song,
that sweetly rings when the night draws near
under the sweetheart's window
(the moon is crawling in velvet darkness)

This was a song
which they were singing
into czars' ears beneath palace windows,
when machine guns wove a speedy death.

And the image vanished,
the sweet voice fell silent.
A touch of snow veiled his sight
and he sees Moscow.

Proud and loud rang out the step,
when below the Kremlin wall
the guards walk to and fro
and terrify Europe and terrify the world.

Then he lifted his eyes from the deep of dreams
and a dry leaf,
torn off the tree by another tree,
descended to earth slowly,

until it fell.

•

Open the windows.
Pain closes the eyes
in the background of red fabrics.

They have lifted the deceased
and the grave is opening.
Dead is Lenin.

The multitudes have stirred.
Step slowly.
The claw of grief will hew.

For the sorrow of the world,
my dear poet,
nightingales sing poorly.

Afterword

(Unless it is perchance for a very technical purpose: filling these last few pages of the book) I don't know why Jaroslav Seifert has an afterword written for a collection sufficiently good as not to need to be covered up by critical loquacity—a collection too precise and clear to require a commentary. It is already beyond the bounds of humility if we must admit that this here will be nothing but an extract of the poet's verses, which may be a decent and more than common feature of insightful essays, but which amounts to a somewhat conspicuous pointlessness in an afterword.

In an afterword to Seifert's book.

Jaroslav Seifert is not and never has been a problem. Neither in terms of merit, nor in terms of intentions. Wherever he was headed, whatever he set his mind on, whatever he had to voice at a given moment, he always expressed it precisely and unequivocally; he never administered the funds of ambiguous mysteriousness. This is why each of his collections—each for these very same reasons self-sufficient and in itself complete—caused the magazines to respond to "a significant turning point in his work." The first one—*City in Tears*—marked the birth of proletarian poetry—of course. The second collection—abandonment of proletarian poetry, embracing of civilization. The third one—rejection of ideology, orientation toward pure poetry, to poetism. The fourth collection—today—a nightingale singing poorly, perhaps indeed something more than a mere fourth in a row, perhaps indeed a turning point, perhaps indeed a case that goes deeper and is more exceptional because it absorbs his entire work and turns him back like a maelstrom into his personal unfathomable center, a point on a straight line into a vortex, on which lies his artistic origin and which he approaches as he deepens his poetic evolution in smaller and smaller circles all the way to the depth of its apex.

Jaroslav Seifert is not and never has been a problem. Perhaps this exonerates those fools who turned him into a schema and whom his clarity and precision, expressing his mental direction in vain, contradict as they undertook to locate in him the romantic, the writer of the idyll, the sensualist servant of anything, fatefully passive, without deliverance.

Why not the opposite? A realist poet, an absolute civilist, who is actively seeking knowledge; why not that which he is, as a full-blooded member of the young generation? An enemy of romanticism, opposed to the idyllic and a relativist only in his dual relationship to the things most dear to him: poetry and social revolution.

This latest collection fully attests to this. It is competent like a final link completing a certain epoch, like the last stop on Seifert's first great journey around the world—travels devoted to familiarization, to expeditions into unknown lands filled with beauty and sorrow.

A Journey Around the World

MOSCOW

The red banner rises above the City in Tears. "There in the east eyes see salvation, there in the east, in the cornflower-blue distance . . ." Moscow is bringing the good tidings of his vision of future justice and beauty. A boyish adventure senses the heroic breath of barricades, of rose-colored death and red resurrection. The sun itself, the entire universe, not even his beloved, are capable of outweighing the idea of revolution.

PARIS

The beloved, after all! Impossible to deny sheer love. Impossible to deny the world and its pleasures; impossible to enter monasteries of renunciation. Secular verse, may it rhyme with Soviet verse. Secular verse. The world! The world? Paris! The antithesis of Moscow, its dreamed-up exclusiveness is the counterweight to the poet's youth. "And, really, Paris is at least one step closer to heavenly spheres . . ." "Paris is the mirror of the world."

ALL THE BEAUTIES OF THE WORLD

Airplanes are soaring from the skies and transatlantic steamers are flooded with the load of poetry. Harbors, the ocean, Marseille and Italy, New York and yachts, skyscrapers, pineapples, all the perfumes of the world, all the beauties of the world, all the nations of the world, blacks, Chinese, poets, steel construction and exotica. The most magnificent journey around the globe on the waves of TSF. "Life swimmers ocean swimmers life and sea life and sea."

ALL THE SORROWS OF THE WORLD

Behind the din of jazz bands, in the shadow of the Eiffel Tower, in the coral lagoon—sorrow. On the bottom of the sea—death. The sorrow of the mayfly, which was born on a rainy day. The sorrow of the wine that is bleeding. "And if it were not for grief love's sickness afflicting me, from which I am dying . . ." Something like war pervades the verses, war and destitution, the menacing weight of all the world's beauty that the poet as discoverer entered. The last nation on earth: *the proletariat.*

And having traveled the globe, he is returning. Lo,

MOSCOW

from whence yesterday he undertook his great expedition seeking knowledge; lo, Moscow, which he left yesterday for the west to find it today coming from the other end, anew and new, entirely different, not the simple play of barricades and red banners, but drudgery, gray work, with rusty blood on the Kremlin wall as a profound trace of necessity and redemption.

This is the history of Jaroslav Seifert's wanderings, his gain, evolution; follow the map of the world that is precise and without obscurities, and mark with tiny pennants the places of his encounters. He undertook a journey around the world and was not belated, the benighted one.

After the waves on TSF we hurled at Seifert the charge of deserting the proletarian cause. We were not right. Not because his poetism could not be placed among bourgeois art, but because *City in Tears* is not fundamentally different. We capitulated in the face of his pure poetry's formal results. We capitulate today faced with his approaching of social unrest. And if the song about all the beauties of the world fades away in this poor singing of the nightingale, if this collection postulates the recognized sorrow of the Earth and its heaviness, it does not mean this is the poetry of TSF at its best, but with its help this is a deepening and intensification of the verses from *City in Tears*.

City in Tears is made of faith, of words and élan. The nightingale sings poorly because it has understood. There he called for deeds and the towering revolutionary wave provided buoyancy. Here knowledge leads. The self-sacrifice of the "Poem Full of Courage" is sweet and boyish. The reserve of the latest verses is bitter and manly. It is the difference between dream and conviction. "On the palm of Europe, where millions crowd," in the name of the throng, the poet today does not renounce a woman "gentle and playful and affectionate of heart." You will not take the revolution's name in vain. It is simpler and more real: "For the idle beauty of foolish women an apple is wasted."

Seifert has become more fervent since learning about the world. He found even today in that gray fog of preparations and agonies which they call consolidation his place as a poet, an uneasy and bitter place. And in his own fate he expressed untheatrically the hopeless lot of intellectuals of his entire generation.

> For the sorrow of the world,
> my dear poet,
> nightingales sing poorly.

That's all!

Julius Fučík

Notes

The following abbreviations are used in the notes below:

Drews = Peter Drews, *Die slawische Avantgarde und der Westen* (Munich: Wilhelm Fink, 1983).

Pešat = Zdeněk Pešat, *Jaroslav Seifert* (Prague: Československý spisovatel, 1991).

Samaltanos = Katia Samaltanos, *Apollinaire: Catalyst for Primitivism, Picabia, and Duchamp* (Ann Arbor, Mich.: UMI Research, 1984).

Šmejkal = František Šmejkal, *Česká výtvarná avantgarda dvacátých let,* exhibition catalog (Prague: Galerie hl. města Prahy, Ústav teorie a dějin umění ČSAV, Uměleckoprůmyslové museum; Brno: Dům umění, 1986?).

Teige = Karel Teige, "Moderní typo," *Typografia* 34, no. 7–9 (1927): 189–98; reprinted in *Svět stavby a básně,* vol. 1 (Prague: Československý spisovatel, 1966), 220–34.

VKS = Jaroslav Seifert, *Všecky krásy světa: Příběhy a vzpomínky* (Cologne: Index, 1981).

CITY IN TEARS

Title
  This collection of poetry, Jaroslav Seifert's first book (1921), was originally entitled *Bojiště dne* [Battlefield of the day].
Dedication
  Seifert dedicated his first collection to his mentor, the poet and journalist Stanislav Kostka Neumann (1875–1947), who helped the young poet to get published and to get a start in journalism.
Foreword
  Signed U. S. Devětsil [Artists Union Devětsil], the prefatory remarks were written by novelist and physician Vladislav Vančura (1891–1942), Seifert's friend and fellow member in the influential avant-garde artistic group Devětsil. During Devětsil's early proletarian phase, it was a trademark for the artists—true to the idea of collective endeavor—to sign the group name or to add Devětsil as a byline.
"December 1920"
  This was a time of strikes and turmoil. Czechoslovakia had emerged as an independent state from the ruins of the Austro-Hungarian Empire two years earlier. In 1920 the Czechoslovak Social Democratic Party began to

split up into a radical (Bolshevik) faction, soon to become communist, and a moderate (Menshevik) wing. The communists tried unsuccessfully to stage a crippling general strike, but violent clashes with police erupted, resulting in several deaths when the police opened fire on the crowds. Seifert most likely witnessed the demonstrations in front of the Parliament in Prague when *Josef Kulda*, a fifty-one-year-old locksmith and father of six, was shot on December 12. Kulda soon succumbed to his injuries.

this word was made flesh, / so that it may dwell among us: John 1:14. This is one of many Scriptural references in *City in Tears*.

"Prayer on the Sidewalk"

gold piece and *sixkreutzer:* I have chosen these words as English-language equivalents of the Czech words *zlatka* and *šesták*. The first, a guilder or gulden, was a coin once current in much of Germany, Austria, and the Netherlands. The second is a small Austrian and German coin, *Sechser* or *Sechsling*, comparable to a sixpenny or nickel.

Fruit Market and Celetná: Two streets in the very center of Prague, near Staroměstské náměstí [Old Town Square]. The reference in the poem is to a life-size effigy of the Virgin Mary that can be found in a niche in the facade of an old patrician house, Dům u černé Matky boží [House at the Black Madonna], on the corner where the two streets intersect.

"Children from the Suburb"

suburb: Unlike the usually wealthy suburbs on the outskirts of cities in the United States, in Prague—as in London—the word "suburb" (*předměstí*) denotes a squalid neighborhood, or even a slum, often located quite close to the town's center, as in the case of Žižkov, Seifert's working-class birthplace.

Maestro Lantner, maker of violins: A well-known Prague manufacturer of string instruments, Ferdinand Lantner. Lantner established his shop in 1862; since 1891, it had been run by his son Bohuslav.

"Revolution"

like Wilde before his judges: Reference to dramatist, poet, novelist, and essayist Oscar Wilde (1856–1900), who was tried for homosexual conduct, found guilty, and spent two years in prison (1895–97).

"Good Tidings"

Ivan Olbracht: Journalist and writer (1882–1952) who worked for the leftist, communist press and Seifert's early mentor. This poem celebrates Olbracht's recent return from postrevolutionary Russia, with "good news" from the country that many leftist intellectuals believed to hold all promise of a more just social order. In its magazine version, this poem was titled "Annunciation."

Glory, / glory to God in the highest / and to his people on earth / revolution: Significant transformation of "Glory to God in the highest and peace to his people on earth" from the Roman Catholic liturgical hymn *Gloria in excelsis Deo.* Seifert substitutes "revolution" for "peace" in a defiant gesture, yet his conception of revolution is more idyllic than ferocious.

"The End of War"

Jerusalem's lake: Seifert makes reference to the New Testament passage John 5:2–9, which describes the healing of the sick in the waters of Bethesda, a small lake or pond north of the Temple in Jerusalem.

"Evening on the Porch"

porch: While it may have a function similar to porches in the United States, here it refers to the galleries or walkways found in the backs of squalid turn-of-the-century working-class tenements in the Žižkov neighborhood, where the residents attended to their household chores but also spent part of their free time.

Šárka: A character from Czech mythology. According to legend, Šárka, the cunning leader of the Czech Amazons, withdraws to the woods and vows revenge on the entire male gender for the infidelity of her lover. The knight Ctirad and his retinue of warriors set out to humiliate and punish the Amazon women. From a distance, they hear the cry of a woman bound to a tree. Not realizing that he is stumbling into a trap, Ctirad is smitten with the woman and liberates her. She offers him and his followers a drink prepared for the purpose, first making them merry and later inducing sleep. She then calls her Amazon sisters, and a bloodbath ensues in which Šárka accomplishes her revenge. The Czech composer Bedřich Smetana (1824–84) wrote a symphonic poem entitled *Šárka,* which became part of the cycle *My Country* (1874–79).

"The Screen at the Cinema"

Procrustes' bed: In Greek legend, Procrustes (also Damastes) was a robber of Attica. He placed his victims upon an iron bed. If they were longer than the bed, he cut off the redundant part; if they were shorter, he stretched them until they fit it. He was slain by Theseus.

Veronica: According to late medieval legend, a woman—who was to become St. Veronica—handed her handkerchief to Jesus on his way to Calvary. After wiping the sweat from his brow, Jesus returned the handkerchief, which bore his exact likeness. Three Italian cathedrals and churches lay claim to the handkerchief.

"In the Garden Gethsemane"

Garden Gethsemane: Matt. 26:36–57; Mark 14:32–53; Luke 22:39–53; John 18:1–13.

seven beautiful virgins: Matt. 25:1–13. A reference to the parable of five prudent virgins who saved and took along lamp oil for the wedding night, as opposed to five who did not, thus signifying the ready anticipation of the Son of God.

"City in Tears"

Jeremiah: The prophet who gave his name to a book in the Old Testament lived in Jerusalem during the time this city fell to the Babylonians. His laments over the fate of Jerusalem can be found in Jer. 15 and elsewhere.

aeroplane: An archaic spelling of the word seems appropriate as Seifert also used an archaic word for airplane.

Mont Blanc or Mount Everest: The highest peak in Europe and the highest mountain on Earth, respectively.

"In a Small Suburban Street"

Jairus's daughter: An afflicted twelve-year-old, thought to be dead, whom Jesus heals (Mark 5:21–43).

In the second edition of *City in Tears* (1923), Seifert inserted a long poem entitled "A Girl" between "A Poem Full of Courage and Faith" and "Poor." The heroine, an unremarkable "generic" revolutionary, is aptly named Marie Nováková. Novák is one of the most common Czech names. In the magazine version, however, the female protagonist bore the name of Seifert's future wife, Ulrychová.

SHEER LOVE

"Poem of Spring" and "New Year's Poem" were eliminated in the second edition of *Sheer Love* (1948).

"Poem of Spring"

and if someone kisses your right cheek, / turn the left one too: A playful variation on a fundamental principle of Christian love.

"Paris"

À Ivan Goll: The poet and journalist Ivan Goll (1891–1950) and his wife Claire (1891–1977), a novelist and poet, maintained contacts with European avant-garde groups, Devětsil among them. The Paris-based Goll was a correspondent for the Croatian avant-garde magazine *Zenit* and wrote in German, French, and English. *Zenit* printed Seifert's poems, and there were personal contacts as well (Drews 249). In his early poetry Ivan Goll was an expressionist; he later became a surrealist. In Switzerland he associated with the Dadaists. He counted James Joyce, Stefan Zweig, and Hans Arp among his friends.

Elbe, Mělník: Mělník is a picturesque town in central Bohemia located on a seven-hundred-foot elevation overlooking the confluence of the rivers Labe (Elbe) and Vltava (Moldau). Prague is situated on the Moldau River.

fiftieth parallel line: Prague's geographical location.

Great Wheel: A ferris wheel.

Trocadéro: The Chaillot Hill overlooking the Seine was named Trocadéro in 1827 in commemoration of the French capture in Spain of a small fortress with the same name. The Palais du Trocadéro, a fanciful, bizarre edifice, was built for the World Exhibition of 1878, but was subsequently razed to make room for the Palais Chaillot in 1937.

Père-Lachaise: A famous cemetery in the north of Paris.

"Hour of Peace"

sordines: From the Italian word *sordino* (pl. *sordini*), a damper on a violin.

"New Year's Poem"

Hugo Stinnes: German industrialist (1870–1924), a symbol of immense wealth, comparable in connotation to members of the Rothschild or Rockefeller families.

Stromovka: A large reserve and game park in the north of Prague, formerly royal gardens established by John of Luxembourg (1296–1346), father of Charles IV.

summer seat: a small fifteenth-century castle overlooking the Stromovka. It served as a hunting lodge during the reign (1576–1611) of Rudolph II (1552–1612), and subsequently, until 1918, it was the summer seat of the Czech vice-regent. The (artificial) *pond* mentioned in the same line refers back to John of Luxembourg, who designed the extensive gardens.

Wenceslas Square: A busy location in the center of Prague where people in Seifert's time would often promenade simply to see and be seen.

Giant Mountains [Krkonoše or Riesengebirge]: Mountain range in northern Bohemia, highest part of the Sudeten Mountains, located in the northern part of today's Czech Republic.

"A Song about Girls"

The piece is the first section of the long poem "A Girl," which Seifert added to the second edition of *City in Tears* (1923).

"Glorious Day"

first of May: Traditional European Labor Day holiday commemorated by leftist parties with marches and demonstrations.

Wenceslas Square [Václavské náměstí]: Long, narrow square in the center of Prague where demonstrations or celebrations have traditionally taken place. In 1989 thousands gathered there during the Velvet Revolution, led by Václav Havel, to topple the communist government.

socio-patriot [*sociálpatriot*]: Pejorative term, used by communists, for Social Democrats.

Third International: The Communist International or Komintern, founded in Moscow in March 1919, was conceived as a world party with separate factions and organized in a strict centralist fashion. It was led by an executive committee in Moscow and its goal was the establishment of the dictatorship of the proletariat and the rule of Soviets. At two congresses in 1921 and 1922, the Komintern, under Lenin and Trotsky, steered a moderate policy to create a unified front along with other leftist parties. After Lenin's death in 1924, however, Stalin abandoned the internationalist policy and pressed for the "leading role" of the Soviet Union, which served him as a justification of expansionist policies.

ducats: Old European gold or silver coins.

carnation: Red carnations and red roses are traditional Social Democratic (and communist) symbols.

"Verses in Remembrance of the Revolution"
The poem refers to the October Revolution of 1917.

to be or not to be, ah, that is the question: A reference to Shakespeare's *Hamlet* that mocks indecision as evidenced in the protagonist's torturous musings (*Hamlet* 3.1).

"Verses about Love, Murder, and the Gallows"
The trip on which the amorous protagonist embarks "for sheer love" is autobiographical. Seifert's future wife came from Jičín, and so the poet knew the town and surrounding country well. In his memoir, Seifert describes his first trip there with his fiancée, and admits that during the second visit he "fell in love" with the town, which was not striking but offered a simple charm: "Nothing extraordinarily great or pathetic, but all was somehow close to the heart" (VKS 355).

Jičín: A small town in eastern Bohemia of approximately 17,000 inhabitants (1991). It boasts a historical center with a town square and a castle dating back to Albrecht von Wallenstein (1583–1634).

statue of Mary: One of several references in this long poem to the statue of the Virgin in Jičín's town square. Such statues or columns can be found in many European squares; often they are of medieval origin, erected in gratitude for deliverance from the plague.

Linden Tree Avenue [Lipová alej]: A long avenue of linden trees leads from Jičín to Libosad. It consists of four rows of trees stretching a length of more than a mile; planted in 1630 by Wallenstein, in Seifert's time it was a favorite meeting place of strolling couples. The tourist guidebooks of Seifert's time capitalized Linden Tree Avenue, although it was not an "official" street. Seifert followed the practice, and so have I.

Libosad: Remnant of Wallenstein's game reserve, a large park with old trees.

Jan Trnka: Seifert here uses a broadside ballad he heard in his childhood, detailing the melodramatic story of the tailor Trnka, who killed his wife for another woman. Trnka was executed by hanging. His lover, distraught because she was not given custody of his five children, committed suicide by jumping down from the town's tower, right in front of the entrance to St. Jacob's Church (VKS 354).

thirteen tinny stars: Seifert, who admits to counting with his fiancée the stars on the gilded halo over the head of this statue of the Virgin Mary, humorously recalls a reader who once wrote to him to correct his count, claiming that there were fourteen stars (VKS 362). The description of the statue changes with the tailor's state of mind.

Zebín: Cone-shaped elevation of approximately 1,200 feet not far from the Linden Tree Avenue. On top was a small chapel of St. Mary Magdalena, surrounded by a cherry orchard that may have been in full bloom, hence "Zebín is flowering pink."

Afterword

Again anonymously signed "Devětsil" and this time written by Karel Teige, Devětsil's chief theoretician, this much-criticized commentary to Seifert's book was once again an expression of group aesthetics. At this time a rift was beginning to develop between adherents of proletarian art and followers of Teige's evolving conception of poetism.

Kladno: A town in central Bohemia of approximately 72,000 inhabitants; concentration of heavy industry, such as coal mines and steel mills.

ON THE WAVES OF TSF

Dedication

The book is dedicated to three innovators: to graphic artist and Devětsil theoretician Karel Teige (1900–1954); to Seifert's fellow poet Vítězslav Nezval (1900–1958); and to founder and director of the avant-garde theater Osvobozené divadlo [Liberated Theater], Jindřich Honzl (1894–1953).

Motto: "Light grief on the face   Deep laughter in the heart"

Provocative, antitraditionalist inversion of famous lines from Czech romantic Karel Hynek Mácha's well-known long poem *Máj* [May], which read "Light smile on the face / deep grief in the heart."

Typography

Conspicuous modernist feature in the tradition of Marinetti's Futurist experiments and Apollinaire's *Calligrammes,* introduced to Seifert's book by Karel Teige, who was an unconventional typographer and designer of many books and magazines in the 1920s. Teige laid down the principles of his designs in several critical articles, foremost among them "Moderní typo" [Modern typography] (1927): "The first concern of modern typography is the *review of type on hand and the selection of fonts that are suitable and correctly designed. A* selection of typefaces *according to the nature of the typeset text* in such a way that *a correspondence between the characteristics of the font and the text* is established, so that the printed form becomes the result of the text's function and content" (Teige 225). It is clear that, like László Moholy-Nagy, Teige saw the printed letter as an important component of expression in its own right. He emphasized, in connection with advertising, that typography is not merely a mediator between content and the reader but "a self-contained construction" that optically arranges the text and "realizes on its basis an optical composition" (Teige 226).

"Guillaume Apollinaire"

Guillaume Apollinaire: French modernist poet, born Wilhelm Apollinaris de Kostrowitski (1880–1918), much admired by the Czech avant-garde for his introduction of simultaneous, polythematic poetry (primarily in his influential long poem *Zône*) and his innovative typography in *Calligrammes.* On the Waves of TSF is suffused with Apollinaire's aesthetic of *l'esprit nouveau,* manifest, among other things, in the nearly complete elimination of punctuation. Apollinaire sustained a head wound in World War I (hence "Your head in white bandages" in line 24) and died of influenza shortly after the Armistice.

Capitalization of personal pronoun, second person singular: Although it may be unusual in English, I emulate a standard polite practice in both Czech and German correspondence. The capitalization is a sign of respect, even reverence, and seems appropriate for Apollinaire.

Étoile: Wordplay referring to the famous square in Paris, Place de l'Étoile, and to the French word for "star," evoking the image of the star of Bethlehem.

sphinx at the Louvre entrance: A reference, apparently, to two effigies of the hybrid mythological figure (half woman, half lion) framing the main entrance to the famous Paris museum.

golden-yellow firecracker: In her book about Apollinaire, Katia Samaltanos quotes the poet Philippe Soupault, who said that Apollinaire was not a leader of a school but what he himself called *une fusée signal* [signal rocket], or catalyst (Samaltanos 64).

"Fiery fruit"

Blaise Cendrars: Pseudonym of Frédéric Sauser, Swiss-born French poet and novelist (1887–1961), known for innovative verse forms and lyrical prose. The American exoticism of his poetry collected in *Kodak* (excerpts of which Karel Čapek included in his 1920 translations from French poetry) may have inspired lines 1–2. The layout of the poem and the use of foreign names also recalls Cendrars's poetry. In the context of "Fiery Fruit," one should note that the pseudonym Blaise Cendrars means roughly "blazing embers." As Samaltanos points out, Cendrars chose light and fire as the symbols of art (109).

Carthage: An ancient city and state which became a dominant colonial and trading power among Phoenician cities in North Africa. It was burned to the ground by the Romans in the Third Punic War (149–146 B.C.).

Miss Muguet: A telling name; *muguet* is the French word for lily of the valley or May lily, a flower that recurs throughout *On the Waves of TSF.*

Perhaps more important, *muguet* can also mean "dandy" and *mugueter* signifies "to flirt." Czech readers in the 1920s were Francophiles and would have been familiar with the word. Seifert used M. Muguet as his pseudonym (Pešat 237).

star: Apparently the Red Star, symbol of the communist revolution often found on top of Soviet buildings.

Bastille: A famous state prison in Paris, seized and sacked by the mob during the French Revolution on July 14, 1789.

Mayakovsky: Vladimir Vladimirovich Mayakovsky (1893–1930), iconoclastic poet of the Russian Revolution.

"Honeymoon"

Wagons lits: The French expression for Pullman cars. Seifert uses banal everyday objects in his poetry as part of his youthful intent to break up poetic conventions.

Wagons restaurants: Railroad dining cars.

"Marseille"

isle of If: The protagonist Edmond Dantès in Alexandre Dumas's novel *Count of Monte Cristo* is confined within the dungeon of the Chateau d'If, located on this island.

Count of Monte Christo: A reference to *Le Comte de Monte Cristo* (1844), a romance by the prolific French novelist and dramatist Alexandre Dumas, père (1802–70). The protagonist is wrongfully imprisoned for life in the dungeon of the Chateau d'If, but manages to escape and to avenge himself. The spelling "Christo" in Seifert's original could be the result of a typographical error; it reappears in the 1992 facsimile edition of *On the Waves of TSF.*

Belsunce: The Cours Belsunce is one of the main streets of Marseille; today it is still a center of entertainment and nightlife.

"Hôtel 'Côte d'Azur' "

Sails / and mint candy: In Czech the phrase for "mint candy" literally means "wind candy" [*větrové bonbóny*].

"My Italy"

Almost certainly a playful reference, particularly in line 6 ("Italian grammar's four irregular verbs see modern poetry"), to Emilio Filippo Tommaso Marinetti (1876–1944) and his radical experiments, particularly the breaking up of syntax, and his "liberated words," *parole in libertà.* The forms *fo* and *vo* do not correspond to modern Italian usage (*faccio* and *vado*, respectively, should be used), and *stano, fano, dano,* and *vano* should be spelled *stanno, fanno, danno,* and *vanno*, but Seifert is less concerned with linguistic precision than with the acoustic and visual quality that these verbs have in Czech.

Forum Romanum: A famous site in Rome that served as a center of commerce and political life in antiquity.

Frappè: Seifert capitalizes the word that bears an Italian accent but comes from the French *frappé,* a drink poured over shaved ice or partly frozen beverages, fruit juices, etc.

garden Boboli: The Boboli Gardens, grounds of the Pitti Palace at Florence, planned in 1550 under the patronage of Eleanora of Toledo and the direction of the sculptor Il Tribolo (Niccolà Pericoli).

"Nightlights"

Ollagums: Seifert uses the Czech plural *Ollagumy,* a brand of condoms available in his youth. Including this word in his poem was definitely a provocation.

"Verses about two who drowned"

Daily-Mail: British daily newspaper. Seifert erroneously hyphenates the name.

"Evening at the café"

Princess Salome: Reference to Oscar Wilde's play *Salomé,* which Seifert may have seen onstage or read in a 1905 translation by Otakar Theer.

"Eccentric"

crown: Czech currency.

"mirror square"

Omaki Vani: Perhaps an imaginary Japanese woman, or a now-forgotten circus or variety artiste whom Seifert encountered on his 1923 trip to France.

Horror shaking the earth and Yokohama in ruins: A reference to a devastating earthquake on September 1, 1923. In the subsequent firestorm, 95 percent of the property in Yokohama was destroyed.

"Miss Gada-Nigi"

Miss Gada-Nigi: Apparently a trapeze artiste and circus dancer, whom Seifert may have seen on his 1923 visit to Paris.

"King Herod"

This poem relies on the similarity in Czech between the grape (*hrozen vína*) that Herod is about to eat and the implied guilt or sin (*vina*) of the female companion addressed by the lyrical "I." It is also a reference to Wilde's play *Salomé.*

"beauty"

manikin: The Czech word *panna* offers greater ambiguity because it also connotes "virgin."

"Discoveries"

The map shown is crucial for the understanding of the poem. Cuba lies at its center, and Seifert emphasizes the fact that he himself does not smoke cigars but cigarettes, so the irreverent poet does not find it important that Columbus discovered the place famous for its cigars. The preoccupation with smoking is typical for Seifert's time.

"Abacus"

apples from Australia: Seifert recalls in his memoir the expensive, beautifully wrapped apples that he used to admire in the delicatessen store windows of his youth (VKS 279).

"New York"

Maiden of Orleans: French national heroine Jeanne d'Arc (1410/12–31) who donned men's clothes and took up arms to lead the French army against the English forces in the Hundred Years' War. She liberated Orléans, which had been under British siege, but was subsequently captured and burned at the stake.

"Napoleon"

Gambier pipe: A clay pipe named after its French inventor and first manufacturer.

"Consolation"

May fly: Dayfly.

"Words on magnet"

Menton: Resort on the French Côte d'Azur near Cap Martin and the last stop before the Italian border on the Marseille–Genoa railway line. Seifert may have passed through on his 1923 trip to Italy and France with Karel Teige.

number two hundred forty-eight: Seifert's original ends with the number one hundred ninety-one, because of the different number of words in the poem. A rhyme is established between *-prvé* in this line and *krve* two lines earlier. I have emulated Seifert's wordplay with the assonance between *-eight* and *bloodstained.*

"!!Hello!!"

magasin Printemps: A beautiful old department store adjacent to the department store complex Galeries Lafayette near the Paris Opera.

mix pleasures like cards and cocktails: In Czech the word for mixing a drink (*míchat*) and shuffling cards is identical.

brothers Fratellini: Three brothers, Albert, Paul, and François Fratellini, well-known circus clowns in Seifert's time. One of them made up his face to look like Pierrot.

boston: A dance in the 1920s; also a game of cards.

"The thief and the clock"

The entire poem relies heavily on homonymy and polysemy. Here in particular Seifert employs the various meanings of *lead* in the sense of guiding but also seducing, as well as in its physical sense of a wire carrying power in a circuit.

Is your piano well-tuned?: The wordplay here relies on the polysemy of the Czech verb *naladit,* which can denote a well-tuned piano and a person in a good mood.

"Concert café"
  This poem was titled "Europe" in its magazine version.
  dreadnought: Seifert employed the English word "dreadnought"
  (battleship) in his Czech original. He often used foreign place names and
  words in this volume to evoke an aura of exoticism and longing for distant
  lands. In his memoirs Seifert mentions observing such a ship in Marseille
  (VKS 162).
"Lawn-tennis"
  Seifert titled his poem in English, again to create an impression of exoticism.
"Cigarette smoke"
  Originally entitled "Kouř v okně" [Smoke in the window], this poem
  reveals an apparent preoccupation with smoking.
  Seifert's friend, the poet František Halas, wrote a short entertaining
  prose piece, "Mám dýmku" [I have a pipe], which extols the pleasures of
  smoking as the "siesta of the mind" (*Pásmo* 2, no. 6–7 [1925–26]: 78).
  Montblanc: Highest peak in the Alps and highest elevation in Europe.
  Also spelled Mont Blanc.
"Fever"
  In its magazine version, this poem was dedicated to Seifert's peer from
  Devětsil's era of proletarian poetry, the poet Jiří Wolker, who died of
  tuberculosis in 1924 at the age of twenty-four.
"Fate"
  Longchamp: Remnants of a former convent of Clare nuns on the west side
  of Paris near the Bois du Boulogne; the convent was secularized and became
  the tryst of the aristocracy; destroyed during the revolution in 1792. In 1861,
  a hippodrome for horse races and military parades was built nearby.
  Your: The pronoun is capitalized in the original to indicate respect or
  adoration. Seifert's capitalization is at times erratic. Often it indicates a
  new thought after a pause, indicated by white spaces.
"Rue de la Paix"
  Rue de la Paix: A well-known street in Paris connecting Place de l'Opera
  and Place Vendôme, the architectural center of the posh district Faubourg
  St.-Honoré.
"To be a fisherman"
  The Czech original thrives on the homonymy of *rýmy*, which in the first
  line of the last stanza means the plural of rhyme and in the third line the
  plural of cold or influenza.

THE NIGHTINGALE SINGS POORLY

Dedication
  Josef Šíma (1891–1971), Czech painter, illustrator, and, like Seifert,
  member of Devětsil. Šíma moved to Paris in 1921, though he retained a

close connection to the Czech avant-garde. He translated Seifert's and Nezval's poems into French (Šmejkal), and provided several illustrations for *The Nightingale Sings Poorly.* The book's cover was created by two other Devětsil painters who were based in Paris: Toyen, alias Marie Čermínová (1902–80) and Jindřich Štýrský (1899–1942), the creators of "artificialism," which was the painterly equivalent of literary poetism—a style of imaginative painting based on association and evocation.

"A Song about Death"
  Wordplay is an important stylistic means in this collection. The original Czech relies on the homonymy of *kosa* (scythe) and *kos* (thrush) in stanza 5, and *závitnice* (spring) and *závistnice* (a female who is envious or aspiring) in stanza 6.

"Ancient Wisdom"
  Archipelago: A reference to Jules Verne's 1884 novel *L'Archipel en feu* [The archipelago on fire]. The associative chain is readily apparent in the Czech: the word for pollen is *pel* (archi*pel*). Verne was much read in Seifert's time.
  The astonishing adventure: Probably a reference to Jules Verne's posthumously published *L'Étonnante aventure de la Mission Barsac* [The astonishing adventure of the Barsac Mission].
  In stanza 5, Seifert uses near homonymy and homophony between profound "wisdom" (*moudrost*) and deep "blueness" (*modrost*). I substituted "deep-seated . . . wisdom" and "deep-sea blueness" to suggest the correspondence that exists in the original.

"14th of July"
  Mirabeau: Comte de Mirabeau (1749–91), French orator and revolutionary leader with early notoriety as a pleasure-seeker, yet his unusual gift for oratory was widely admired. One of the most important figures in the first two years of the French Revolution.
  July fourteenth: Bastille Day.
  In stanza 4, the associative leap from "bars" to "colors" is playfully obvious in the Czech original: *bary* to *barvy.*
  cap of liberty: Seifert uses the phrase "Phrygian cap," that is, the *bonnet rouge* worn by French revolutionaries, who in turn adopted the liberty cap that designated freed Roman slaves.
  calembour: The French word means pun or wordplay; it has entered the Czech language as *kalanbur.*

"Girlfriends"
  Gisèle and Emma: Probably a reference to Gustave Flaubert's (1821–80) protagonist Emma Bovary and to the ballet *Gisèle.*
  Mr. Amundsen: Norwegian polar explorer Roald Amundsen (1872–1928), who visited Prague in 1925 on a lecture tour. His book *To the North Pole by Plane,* documenting his 1925 journey, was publicized in the Czech

press. Several poets wrote pieces commemorating Amundsen's expeditions.

"Paravent"

French for folding screen; the word entered the Czech language in phonetic spelling: *paraván.*

lemon eyes: Perhaps suggestive of a yellow European butterfly like the brimstone (*Gonepteryx rhamni*), which is called *Zitronenfalter* in German (lemon butterfly).

"Panorama"

In Czech the word for summit or crest is identical with comb (*hřeben*).

"Giant Mountains"

Krakonoš: Mythic figure of Bohemian folklore, comparable to Paul Bunyan; believed to have superhuman powers and to roam the Giant Mountains.

"Bread and Roses"

cornet: Seifert here apparently alludes to the cone shape and probable origin of the dicebox: the musical instrument cornet or horn. It was customary for soldiers to play games of chance on overturned drums.

"Old Battlefield"

danseuse: The French word does not appear in the original but seems appropriate to denote a *female* dancer (*tanečnice* in Czech).

"A Ballad from the Champagne"

It is likely that this poem is a reference to Apollinaire's poem "Vigneron champenois" from *Calligrammes* because of its linkage of vineyard and war theater. The epigraph was probably a headline taken from the French magazine *Le Temps.* The Czech magazine *Republika* quotes a lower number, citing French sources: 400 French men of letters killed in World War I (*Republika*, February 26, 1919, 23).

Josephine: While the association with Napoleon's wife comes readily to mind, it is more likely that Seifert was looking for a "generic" or typical French female name.

"Three Bitter Seeds"

Dedication: Konstantin Biebl (1898–1951), Seifert's poet friend and fellow member of Devětsil since 1926, when Biebl likewise embraced poetism. Longing for exotic faraway places, particularly Asia (where he actually traveled), increasingly informed his poetry.

Section III, the last part of this volume, is a cycle of poems Seifert wrote following his visit in 1925 to Moscow and Leningrad.

collier: French word for necklace, usually made of precious stones or pearls.

orb: The Czech word for "orb" is the same as for "apple"; therefore, it is more readily apparent why this emblem of authority is worm-eaten and rotten.

"At Our Lady of Iberia"

Our Lady of Iberia: A chapel, Časovnja Iverskoj Božej Materi, built in 1669 adjacent to the Iberian Gates, Iverskie vorota, which opened onto the Red Square in Moscow. The magazine version of this poem reveals in a note that the chapel served as an antireligious monument in atheist postrevolutionary Russia, bearing Marx's motto "Religion—the opiate of the people." Nearby, there was a lively bazaar. Both the chapel and the gates were destroyed in the late 1920s. The chapel held the icon of the Iberian Virgin, much venerated by Muscovites. In ancient geography, Iberia was a country between the Greater Caucasus and Armenia, roughly equivalent to modern Eastern Georgia.

"Lenin"

The poem commemorates the death, on January 21, 1924, of Russian statesman and communist leader Vladimir Ilyich Lenin.

Afterword

Written by communist critic and journalist Julius Fučík (1903–43), long a detractor of poetism, who briefly "converted" to this aesthetic in 1926. In the last section, entitled "Moscow," the sentence "He undertook a journey around the world and was not belated, the benighted one" involves a wordplay in Czech: *nezpozdil* and *zpozdilý* for "belated" and "benighted." This likely refers to Jules Verne's novel *Around the World in Eighty Days,* as Fučík's afterword does on more than one occasion. Verne was a much admired and widely read writer in Czechoslovakia. At the same time, Fučík gently mocks Seifert's unworldly innocence ("benighted"). The reference toward the end to *consolidation,* "that gray fog of preparations and agonies," is directed against the mainstream parties' and the young Czechoslovak state's stabilization, hold on power, and strengthened position in the second half of the 1920s, a development disliked by communists who sought to destabilize the "bourgeois" democratic system.